Mario S. Catalani · Giuseppe F. Clerico

Decision Making Structures

Dealing with Uncertainty within Organizations

With 15 Figures

Physica-Verlag

A Springer-Verlag Company

Series Editors
Werner A. Müller
Peter Schuster

Authors
Dr. Mario S. Catalani
Dr. Giuseppe F. Clerico
Department of Economics
University of Torino
Via Po 53
I-10124 Torino, Italy

Die Deutsche Bibliothek - CIP-Einheitsaufnahme

Decision making structures : dealing with uncertainty within organizations / Mario S. Catalani ; Giuseppe F. Clerico. - Heidelberg : Physica-Verl., 1996
  (Contributions to management sciences)
  ISBN 3-7908-0895-4
NE: Catalani, Mario S.; Clerico, Giuseppe F.

Printed with a contribution of the Universitá degli Studi di Torino, Dipartimento di Economia

ISBN 3-7908-0895-4 Physica-Verlag Heidelberg

This work is subject to copyright. All rights are reserved, whether the whole or part of the material is concerned, specifically the rights of translation, reprinting, reuse of illustrations, recitation, broadcasting, reproduction on microfilm or in any other way, and storage in data banks. Duplication of this publication or parts thereof is permitted only under the provisions of the German Copyright Law of September 9, 1965, in its current version, and permission for use must always be obtained from Springer-Verlag. Violations are liable for prosecution under the German Copyright Law.

© Department of Economics, University of Torino 1996
Printed in Germany

The use of general descriptive names, registered names, trademarks, etc. in this publication does not imply, even in the absence of a specific statement, that such names are exempt from the relevant protective laws and regulations and therefore free for general use.

SPIN 10522478   88/2202 - 5 4 3 2 1 0 – Printed on acid-free paper

PREFACE

This book is the culmination of many years' research inspired by the pioneering and seminal works of Sah and Stiglitz. We gratefully acknowledge the influence of these two authors, whose ideas and contributions have brought us together on this collaboration, despite our divergent scientific backgrounds (while Catalani is interested in quantitative methods, Clerico is a non-quantitative economist).

We thank the Editor of the *Rivista Internazionale di Scienze Economiche e Commerciali* for permission to use slightly modified versions of papers published in that Review (they are the content of Chapters I and III of Part I, and of Chapter I of Part II).

We heartily thank Ms. Laura McLean for carefully revising our English.

The publication of this book has been made possible by a grant from the Department of Economics, University of Turin, Italy.

Torino, July 1995

Mario S. Catalani

Giuseppe F. Clerico

CONTENTS

Introduction   1

PART I
Some models of decision making structures

I.	How and when unanimity is a superior decision rule	15
II.	Majority rules and efficiency of the decision process	31
III.	Team cooperation vs. independent assessment	41
IV.	Leadership and dependence	59
V.	The decision making process of political organizations	75

PART II
Pyramid decision structures

I.	Pyramidal structures: a preliminary note	91
II.	Other properties of pyramids	103
III.	Pyramids and dependence	117
IV.	Organization, loyalty, and efficiency	133

Conclusions   151

References   163

Mario S. Catalani is the sole author of the Appendices and of Part I Chapter IV and Part II Chapters II and III.

NOTE TO THE SYMBOLOGY

The following notation is used throughout this book.

$\mathcal{B}(n, p)$ denotes a binomial random variable with n trials and probability of success p.

$\tau(p)$ is the waiting time for the first success in Bernoulli trials with probability of success p; when specified, this variable is stopped at time n.

$\mathbf{E}[X]$ denotes the expected value of the random variable X.

$\mathbf{V}ar[X]$ denotes the variance of the random variable X.

$\mathbf{C}ov[X, Y]$ denotes the covariance between the random variables X and Y.

$\mathbf{P}r[A]$ denotes the probability of the event A.

Other operators and random variables are defined in the text.

INTRODUCTION

THE FALLIBILITY OF HUMAN ORGANIZATIONS

This Introduction does not aim to present an overall review of the literature on the problems related to the decision process of organizations nor to provide an exhaustive survey of the issues inherent to such problems. Neither does it offer the reader any discussion on the nature or source of human fallibility. Instead it intends to describe the context into which our analysis of the decision processes and of the decision making organizations will be fitted.

"...Organizations are systems of coordinated action among individuals and groups whose preferences, information, interests, or knowledge differ. Organization theories describe the delicate conversion of conflict into cooperation, the mobilization of resources and the coordination of effort that facilitate the joint survival of an organization and its members." (March and Simon, 1993, p. 2).

This book presents some stylised models of organizations focusing on the decision making process and the conditions that can guarantee its "optimality".

Our analysis begins with the consideration that, in general, the quality of individual human decisions essentially depends on the following variables: incomplete information, uncertainty, quality of human capital, time required to reach the decision, and the degree of individual identification with the pursued goal. These variables act as inputs, entailing costs, of a production process whose output is the decision. Better information is usually achieved through a gathering process that implies a greater amount of time. The quality of the output improves as the quality of the inputs improves. But increasing the quality of the inputs implies greater costs. Thus, the improved output quality must be examined in relation to the higher cost of the inputs.

As each of the above mentioned variables entails a cost, we can say that all human decisions are fallible, given the resource scarcity. While it is theoretically possible to improve the quality of a decision by infinitely increasing the possessed information and the quality of human capital, in reality this is not feasible given the constraint on resources. Fallibility arises as a consequence of a necessarily limited mix of inputs.

The same variables affecting the quality of an individual's decision making are also involved in the decision process of a group of people organized in a decision structure (hereafter also referred to as an organization). At work in this case are other variables which depend on the specific form of the organization. Within any given organization the quality of the decision is influenced by two additional factors: the adopted decision rule and the nature of the relationships among the individuals belonging to the organization. The variables "time required to reach a decision" and "degree of identification with the pursued goal" as applied to the organization's decision process can be interpreted as the degree of the loyalty of the members towards the goal pursued by the organization. A higher degree of loyalty entails a greater individual effort, resulting in a reduction of the time required to make a decision. In other words, higher loyalty means a contraction of the phenomena of laziness and shirking.

To sum up, we make the following assumptions in our analysis of organizational decision making:

1. Every human decision is subject to error.

2. The quality of decisions is affected by the form of the organization.

3. The quality of decisions is affected by the adopted decision rule.

4. The quality of decisions is affected by the nature of the relationship among the individuals within the organization.

5. The quality of decisions is affected by the level of loyalty of the members of an organization.

1. Human fallibility

We have modeled the variables incomplete information and uncertainty using a probabilistic approach. To simplify our analysis, we have confined ourselves to examining the case of a dichotomous choice, for example, whether to accept or to reject an industrial project, whether or not to enact a law, whether or not to amend a Charter, or whether to convict or to acquit a defendant. The probabilistic approach implies that the individual decision process can be simulated by the toss of a coin, where the probability of success reflects the possessed information and the degree of uncertainty. Statistical decision theory allows us to describe the outcome of a decision process in the following way. To each state of the world there corresponds only one right decision, and we can assign a probability to the making of this decision. For instance, the state of the world might be represented by a portfolio of industrial projects composed of profitable and unprofitable projects. We can refer to the rejection of a profitable project as *error of the first type* and the acceptance of an unprofitable project as *error of the second type*. Then let α be the probability of the type I error and β be the probability of the type II error. Typically, each decision corresponding to a particular state of the world is associated to a payoff (positive or negative, according to whether the decision is correct or incorrect). In our general framework we have also attributed probabilities to each state of the world. Pursuing the example, this implies that the proportion of profitable projects belonging to the portfolio is known. In our probabilistic scheme, the probability of making the right decision can be considered as a measure of the *skills* (quality of the human capital) of the decisor and of the information possessed by the decisor. Improved quality of human capital and/or more precise information thus increases the probability of making the right decision. However, both these improvements entail a cost, the net payoff resulting from the correct decision must likewise be reduced. It is clear from this approach that we can derive the expected net payoff associated to decisions for each state of the world. Using the a-priori likelihood of each state of the world, it is thus possible to associate to each decision its expected net payoff depending on the following parameters: the probabilities of the two types of error, the payoff matrix of the outcome, and the a-priori probabilities of the states of the world.

The same analysis applies when the decisor is an organization made up of n individuals. The starting point would be the individuals who possess given skills and given information; as before this means that they are characterized by having a given probability to make type I and type II errors (not necessarily equal). The choice made by an organization results from the choices made by its members; the nature of this result is a topic extensively analysed in the book. The result depends primarily on two factors: the architecture of the organization (that is the relations among members in the organization) and the majority rules followed in making a decision. The term "architecture" is borrowed from Sah and Stiglitz, whose work has deeply influenced our research (Sah and Stiglitz 1985, 1986, 1988a, 1988b, Sah 1991). We will demonstrate that these two factors, coupled with the degree of dependence among members (if and how a decision of a member is influenced by the decision of another member), determine the α and β values of the organization.

2. The architecture of organizations

Three elementary forms of organizational structures can be identified: hierarchy, polyarchy and committee.

In order to characterize these structures it is useful to consider how each performs the task of evaluating a project drawn from a portfolio of projects. Again only dichotomous choices will be examined. For purpose of analysis we make the following assumptions.

i) Each organization is composed of at least two members.

ii) All members are aware of the portfolio composition in profitable and unprofitable projects.

iii) Each member shares the same information.

iv) The members are homogeneous with respect to their skills.

v) Each member acts independently from the others.

2.1 *Hierarchy*

Hierarchy is a decision structure composed of n levels (where $n =$ number of the members). The evaluation process begins at the first or bottom level. If the project is accepted at the bottom level, it then passes to assessment by the second level; otherwise, the project is discarded from the portfolio. So with the exception of the bottom level, each level can assess a project only if the previous level has accepted it. A project is only accepted by the decision structure once the n decision levels have accepted it. This very simple mechanism (built on simplifying assumptions) can also be employed to describe more complicated and articulated situations. For instance the decision process of structures organized on the decentralization of both information and of information processing is the same as that described above. The decentralization of information means that "different decision makers in the firm will typically have different information" (Radner, 1992, p. 1384). Decentralization of information processing means that the task of processing of information is shared by many people within the organization.

The hierarchical organization so far described implies that the decision power delegation stems down from the top level. As one moves from the bottom to the top level of a hierarchy the workload actually decreases while decision making power on more important (strategic) problems increases. In fact, the top level is concerned with only strategic issues. Consequently the top level has the power to delegate power and to assign the workload to the lower hierarchical levels, and has the power of definitive choice on projects submitted by the hierarchical levels.

2.2 *Polyarchy*

Polyarchy is a decision structure made up of n members organized such that projects are evaluated in parallel, as opposed to the implicit serial fashion of the hierarchy. All the members are situated at the same level. A project drawn from the project portfolio comes to the assessment of one member of the polyarchy, who can accept or reject the project. If he accepts it, the project is accepted by the organization. Otherwise, if the project is rejected, it is returned to the portfolio and another member of the polyarchy can redraw the project and reassess it with no knowledge of the former rejection. Consequently, the polyarchy accepts a project when anyone of its members accepts it. In contrast to hierarchical organization where there is delegation of power from the top to the bottom levels and, consequently, different degrees of power at different levels, the polyarchy entails a complete decentralization of power: each member is equally powerful. The workload in the polyarchy is more uniformly distributed, and the organization implies a lesser amount of screening of projects.

2.3 *Committee*

A committee is a decision structure whose n members make decisions jointly and simultaneously. Based on the assumptions stated at the beginning of this Section there is no leader in the elementary form of a committee, and all the members are similar. A committee is characterized by majority rule (simple majority, qualified majority, etc.) in decision making. Such a majority rule can be referred to as the consensus level of the committee.

In a less rigorous analysis, we can examine other elements of the decision process of a committee, including the presence and the role of a leader within the organisation, the interdependence among members, and the time required to reach a decision given the decision rule. We present a more thorough discussion of these topics in Section 3 of this Introduction.

2.4 *A comparison of the three elementary forms*

An additional factor which we have not yet discussed is the problem of cooperation among the decisors: this will be dealt with in a later chapter.

From a probabilistic point of view the three forms of decision structures can be characterized as follows.

i) In a hierarchy a project is accepted if all the members accept it.

ii) In a polyarchy a project is accepted if at least one member accepts it.

iii) In a committee a project is accepted if at least k members have accepted it, where k represents the required consensus level.

From this point of view, a hierarchy is a committee with $k = n$, and a polyarchy is a committee with $k = 1$.

Given our assumptions, the probability that the decision structure accepts a project is calculated simply by using the binomial distribution, where the probability of success is the individual probability of accepting the project. This simple but powerful analytical scheme allowed Sah and Stiglitz to study the determination of the optimal consensus level for a committee, considering the number of members, the skills of the members and the portfolio's composition as parameters. In order to further compare the three forms, it is worthwhile to introduce a new factor: the quality of the portfolio. The quality of the portfolio is defined as the expected value of the benefit of a project randomly drawn from a portfolio having a given composition of profitable and unprofitable projects. When this expected value is equal to zero we can say that the portfolio's quality is neutral, that is, the positive expected benefit equals the negative expected benefit. Where the expected value is greater than zero we can define the quality as good. If the expected value is negative the quality is considered bad.

By using the binomial distribution it is easy to rank the three elementary forms in decreasing level of probability to accept a project (whether profitable or unprofitable): polyarchy, committee (with a consensus level strictly greater than one and lesser than n), hierarchy.

In the presence of a high quality portfolio, it is desirable to have higher probabilities of acceptance of a project. Consequently we can conclude that the higher the portfolio's quality, the higher the performance of a polyarchy with respect to that of a committee, and the higher the performance of a committee with respect to that of a hierarchy.

To expand our analysis let us assume that each single evaluation of a project entails a cost. There is a fundamental difference between the expected evaluation cost per project for a committee on the one hand and for a polyarchy or for a hierarchy on the other. In a committee, evaluations are simultaneous, while in both a polyarchy and in a hierarchy evaluations follow specific sequential patterns; thus, there is a greater number of evaluations involved in the committee decision process than that of either a polyarchy or a hierarchy. This leads to the conclusion that "... The relative performance of a hierarchy or of polyarchy improves, compared to that of a committee, if evaluations are costlier" (Sah and Stiglitz, 1988b, p. 463).

The economic literature on the analysis of the three elementary forms touches on another aspect involved: the total time required by each organisation to make a decision. Sequential decision structures generally entail incremental time delays. These time delays sometimes prove crucial, since, as Sah and Stiglitz (1988b, p.466) have said, "... The economic cost of time delays is not only a reduction (due to discounting) in the present value of projects undertaken, but also a possible reduction in the value of projects due to competitors' actions (e.g. in patent races)." Since the additional cost entailed by a time delay is proportional to the length of the sequence of assessments through which a project must pass, it is obvious that the committee presents the smallest time delay cost. The highest time delay cost is found in the case of a hierarchy, while polyarchy is located in between these two extremes. The issue of time delay cost will be extensively analysed in this book.

2.5 *A proposed model: pyramidal organizations*

In the second part of this book we propose a model of organisation which is a mix of the elementary forms of hierarchy and polyarchy. This new decision structure is referred to as the pyramid decision structure.

All the members belonging to this type of organisation are distributed in a series of levels (piers), each consisting of a number of members not greater that that of the level immediately below. Each level behaves as a polyarchy, that is, a project is accepted if and only if at least one of its members accepts it. Yet the overall organization functions as a hierarchy, that is, it accepts a project if and only if all the levels have accepted it.

Given the total number of members belonging to this type of organisation and the number of levels, we have many possible distributions of members across the levels, respecting the requirement of the pyramid structure. We refer to these different distributions as the different configurations of the pyramid. In this organisation we introduce a *quasi-lexicographic* ordering of configurations which can be considered as a sort of law of evolution from an originary configuration. From a dynamic point of view, this ordering can be stated in the following way: from each configuration the next one is obtained through the movement of one member from the bottom level to that immediately above (the second level), so long as the resulting configuration is still a pyramid. If this is not possible, then we may see a movement of one member from the second level to the third one, and so on.

The aim is, given the total number of members and the number of levels of this organisation, to compare the different configurations with respect to their performance measured by the accuracy of the made decision and the time delay cost as described at the end of the previous subsection. We will see that this ranking of configurations is consistent with a decreasing ranking of the loyalty of the members.

3. Decision rules

The following discussion is understood in the context of a committee as described in Section 2. Let us recall that the characteristic feature of a committee is that the members must jointly and simultaneously make a dichotomous decision according to a given consensus level. We will focus on two issues: the time required to make a decision when the consensus level is not the simple majority, and the interdependence of members.

As for the first problem, if the consensus level is not the simple majority, there exists a positive probability that the committee will not reach the required majority. In this case it will be necessary to reconvene the committee, and perhaps to reconvene it again and again until the required majority is reached. In this case the additional time necessary to make a decision implies a cost that we call the transaction cost of the decision structure. This cost increases with the number of meetings required by the committee. So the expected total cost of the committee can be divided into two elements: the expected cost related to the correctness of the made decision, and the cost of the expected time necessary to reach the decision. The problem is then to determine the consensus level which would minimize the expected total cost.

As for the second problem, we are going to consider two sources of dependence among the members. The first is due to the presence of a leader, whose special position is characterised by a higher attainment of skills and the recognition of such by the residual members. The leader's presence influences the other members' decision. The second source of dependence arises from the common *Weltanschauung* of the members. In the case of political organisations, the members of the decision structure share a common ideology.

An early discussion of the problems of this section can be found in Condorcet's *Essai* of 1785, in which he presents a mathematical analysis of the deliberative process of assemblies. Two of his results seem to us particularly cogent: first, the possibility of cyclical majorities; and second, what is now known as the *Condorcet jury theorem*. "The Condorcet jury theorem says that if each individual is somewhat more likely than not to make the 'better' choice between some pairs of alternatives -along some specified evaluation dimension- and each individual has the same probability of being correct in his choice, then under independent voting the probability that the group majority is correct is greater than the individual probability. Moreover, the probability of a correct decision increases towards a limiting value of 1, as the number of individuals increases." (Berg, 1993b, p. 437-438)... "There is an obvious conceptual relationship between Condorcet's jury theorem and Rousseau's work; Rousseau and Condorcet approached decision-making in essentially the same manner. Both regarded voting not merely as a device to ascertain the will of the strongest party within an assembly, but essentially as a means of ensuring the emergence of an enlightened decision from the majority vote. The general will (Rousseau's *volonté générale*) is to be ascertained by voting, an understanding of the process of voting not as a means of combining divergent interests, but rather as process that searches for 'truth'." (Berg, 1993b, p. 438).

4. How the book is organised

In Part I of this work we present some models of decision making structures. In Part II we present our model of pyramid decision organizations.

Part I.
In Chapter I and Chapter II we discuss how and when special majority rules are advantageous. In general, a special majority rule entails more time than the simple majority rule in reaching decision. In Chapter I we model this additional time by means of the process by which the leader influences the other members' choice. In Chapter II this additional time is measured by the number of times it is necessary to reconvene the decision structure. We show that, in both models, the determination of the most advantageous majority rule rests on the ratio between the cost due to the delay and the cost associated to the wrong decision. The advantage of more stringent majority rules increases when that ratio decreases.
In Chapter III we outline the owner's dilemma in confronting the performance of two decision organisations: one composed of members acting independently, the other one made up of members working together cooperatively in the presence of a leader. In the latter model the other variable which must be taken into account is the additional salary required to employ the leader.
Chapter IV is essentially an extension of Condorcet's jury theorem, although the assumption of independence among the members is less rigid and the members are allowed to be non-homogeneous. Conditional independence is the probabilistic tool used in modelling. Here, too, the correlation among members is studied in the presence of a Leader and the distribution of the number of votes of the same type is examined. It is demonstrated that, in the range of values relevant to our parameters, this distribution is bimodal.
In Chapter V we present a model that particularly well suits the decision process followed by political organisations and parties whose members share a common ideological background. It examines the effect of the introduction of dependence both on the probability to make the right decision as well as on the expected number of evaluations a project must pass before a decision is made. Dependence is introduced through the scheme of the Polya-Eggenberger's urn model. One parameter of this model can be assumed to represent

the measure of the dependence.

Part II.

In Chapter I and II we introduce our proposed model of pyramidal organisations, maintaining the basic assumptions given at the start of Section 2. Given the total number of members and the number of levels of the pyramid, we consider the different resulting configurations, that is the different distribution of members across the levels which still respects the rule characterising a pyramid. We formulate a law of evolution by which these configurations can be *genetically* ordered, that is, moving from a configuration that can be considered as the originary one up to a configuration that can be considered stable. The first result is a formula for determining the number of possible configurations. The different configurations are then compared with respect to the probability of making the correct decision, and the expected time necessary to reach that decision.

In Chapter III, the analysis of pyramidal organisations is extended, relaxing some of the above mentioned basic assumptions. Essentially, we introduce three different models of dependence. In the first model, the intensity of each member's effort is variable, depending on the degree of loyalty of the members to the entire structure (a concept more extensively developed in Chapter IV). A second model makes individual skills variable and, finally, a third model makes the composition of each level variable, while still respecting the pyramid rule. An application is then offered.

In Chapter IV we show that it is possible to make each configuration correspond to the degree of loyalty as inferred from the member's individual effort in response to promotion possibilities inside the pyramidal organisation. The higher these possibilities, the higher is the member's effort and the more intense is his identification with the organisation's goals. In our model the level of effort is a measure of loyalty. Pyramidal organisations aim to maximise the efficiency of the decision process. Efficiency is defined as a combination of the correctness and the velocity of the decision. The aim of this Chapter is to compare the efficiency level of the different configurations, keeping in mind that a specific degree of loyalty corresponds to each configuration, and hence, with a specific degree of swiftness in making the decision.

PART I

SOME MODELS OF DECISION MAKING STRUCTURES

CHAPTER I

HOW AND WHEN UNANIMITY IS A SUPERIOR DECISION RULE †

1. Introduction

The kind of problems we are going to deal with can be described briefly as follows.

a) Any body whose task is to make decisions among alternatives may follow different procedural rules such as simple majority, special (or qualified) majority and unanimity.

b) The decision process involves different types of uncertainty including the state of the world, human fallibility, and the asymmetry of information.

c) The outcome of each decision process is affected by a cost associated to the making of a wrong decision, the *error cost*. To this

---

† Reprinted, with slight modifications, from *Riv. Inter. di Scienze Economiche e Commerciali*, 1-2, 1995.

cost must be added a cost associated to the specific procedural rule in force, the *specific cost*. The *total cost* associated to each decision is equal to the sum of these two costs.

d) One way to formally introduce uncertainty is to model the behavior of each member of the organization probabilistically. More precisely, each individual has a definite probability of making the correct decision, depending on their skill. We must emphasize that this probabilistic setup, and even the analytical development, follows the approach taken by Sah and Stiglitz (1985, 1986, 1988a, 1988b) and Sah (1991) to tackle a related problem. In their papers, they "... study the decision making of committees and contrast this to the decision making of certain stylized forms of centralized versus decentralized organizations..." (Sah and Stiglitz, 1988; p. 451). The centralized organizations are identified as hierarchies and the decentralized ones as polyarchies.

e) If the foregoing assumptions are accepted, it seems worthwhile to ask whether and how different procedural rules affect the decision costs, so as to ascertain under which conditions one procedural rule might be better than others. More precisely, the question is whether and when a procedural rule exists which minimizes the total cost of each decision.

The present chapter aims to formalize this type of problem, and to illucidate the existence of the conditions mentioned under e).

2. Some insights from the literature

We consider a group of persons (say n) whose task it is to reach a decision about a proposed project. Our stylized model assumes that the decision is dichotomous, that is, either to accept or reject the project. Abstention is not allowed. The project is randomly selected from a portfolio of projects containing a proportion π percent of good projects. The group members are fallible, and can make two types of error: type I error is rejecting a good project and type II error is accepting a bad project. Generally, the probability of type I error and the probability of type II error vary across the members of the decision group. We denote with $1 - p_i$ and q_i, respectively, these two probabilities for the i-th member. The complement to one of each of these probabilities may be considered as a measure of individual skills. We assume that there is a cost c_1 for rejecting a good project and a cost c_2 for accepting a bad project. In the case of a correct decision the cost is equal to zero. In this way we can construct a payoff matrix associated to decisions. Every member of the decision group aims to minimize the costs associated with the decision made. Members do not pursue selfish goals; therefore we do not deal with the logrolling phenomenon.

The problem to be considered is to determine how different majority rules affect this cost. For a simpler framework which does not distinguish between the two types of errors, but which simply speaks of an incorrect decision and which deals with a symmetric payoff matrix, the literature has established a definite result: the decision rule which maximizes the probability of a group to reach the correct judgment is a majority weighted voting rule (Nitzan and Paroush, 1984; Shapley and Grofman, 1984). In the case of an asymmetric payoffs matrix, "it makes sense to slant the decision procedure ... A good corporate example may be the imposition of a significant special majority requirement in cases of 'important' decisions, such as mergers, liquidations, or charter amendments." (Nitzan and Procaccia, 1986; p. 198).

To sum up, the general framework for studying this kind of problem is characterized by the following variables: the individual skills of each manager; the number n of members; the payoffs associated, in any state of the world, with the made decision; and the objective prior likelihood of each state of the world.

3. Unanimity versus simple majority

Let us imagine a situation in which a committee features a minority of old members and a majority of younger ones. The old members hold the committee's leadership due to their past experience. When unanimity is required we assume that the leadership will impose its will. There will be two different types of projects under scrutiny : the *conventional* and the *unconventional* ones. A conventional project is a project which is homogeneous to those examined in the past. We are interested in analysing the relative performance of two majority rules (unanimity versus simple majority) both in conventional and unconventional projects. Performance is measured by the expected total cost associated to the decision made. The total cost includes two items: *i* the costs related to the two types of errors (as described in Section 2) which may be called the *error cost*; *ii* the cost related to the specific majority rule in force, that is the *specific cost*.

We assume that the the skills of the old and young members of the committee are different, but homogeneous within each group. In our model the skills of the old members are denoted with the subscript 1, and the skills of the young ones with the subscript 2.

For a conventional project we assume that the old members have better skills. Using the previous notation we can write

$$p_1 > p_2, \qquad q_1 < q_2.$$

On the contrary, we can imagine that younger members are better equipped to deal with new and unconventional situations, which means

$$p_1 < p_2, \qquad q_1 > q_2.$$

When the committee examines a conventional project, unanimity rule entails a specific cost given by the time necessary to reach unanimity, while simple majority rule does not entail any specific cost.

In the case of unconventional projects the majority (young members) feels itself to possess, and indeed does possess, better skills. Consequently they feel that the leadership (represented by the old members) is a burden and so they are motivated to get rid of it. This implies replacing the existing decision structure with a new one. The development of this new decision structure entails a cost. The only way to avoid this situation is to constrain the decision process by the unanimity rule. In this context the simple majority rule has a specific cost (resulting from the collapse of the existing decision structure) which is absent when unanimity is required.

In what follows we first present a model of the process by which unanimity is reached when the committee faces a conventional project, formalizing the specific cost of unanimity in this situation. We do not formalize the specific cost of simple majority rule in the second situation presented (unconventional project).

Nevertheless, it is still possible to compare the dynamics of the relative performance of the two majority rules within the two contexts.

4. The model

To simplify the problem we assume a decision structure (say a board) formed by three managers. Thus we do not consider the number of managers a parameter of our model, and consequently the wage of each manager does not enter the cost of the decision process. Let the project be a conventional one. The members are not homogeneous as there exists a member possessing a higher level of skills than the other two, who have similar skills. Initially, each manager forms his opinion about the decision to be made independently of his peers.

When simple majority is required, a decision is immediately reached since $n = 3$. In the case of unanimity, however, the board may initially be split. We therefore need to model the discussion process through which unanimity is reached.

The cost entailed by the time spent in the discussion process characterizes this kind of majority rule. We choose to model this process as a Markov Chain with the following properties.
1) The manager possessing the highest degree of skills is able to influence the decision of the other two managers; the outcome is that the board will vote according to his opinion.
2) The members who are influenced do not influence each other, and change their opinion according to a common probabilistic law represented by *transition probabilities* which are strictly greater than zero and less than one. Let φ be the probability to stick to an original opinion. It is reasonable to make φ dependent on the strength of the leadership.

An easy way to do this is then to write

$$\varphi = 1 - (p_1 - p_2).$$

While under these assumptions unanimity is assured sooner or later, the required time is a random variable. The expected value of this time can be used as a measure of the discussion cost, which is the *specific cost* of unanimity.

In the case of simple majority in our model the *specific cost* is equal to zero.

The *error cost* is, in both situations, equal to c_1 (for the rejection of a good project) or c_2 (for the acceptance of a bad project).

For the sake of convenience, we hereafter assume that the project under discussion is a good one.

Let γ_1 and γ_2 be the *total cost* respectively of unanimity and of simple majority. As shown in the Appendix

$$\gamma_1 = \mathbf{E}[\tau_G] + c_1(1 - p_1),$$

where $\mathbf{E}[\tau_G]$ is the expected time spent to reach unanimity,

$$\gamma_2 = c_1(1 - p_2)(1 + p_2 - 2p_1 p_2).$$

So we have to study the behavior of

$$\Delta = \gamma_1 - \gamma_2,$$

for changes in the parameters of the model.

Clearly, $\Delta < 0$ implies that unanimity is the better choice. Now let $c_1^\star > 0$ be the cost such that $\Delta = 0$, that is the indifference cost of the two majority rules. Then
i) if

$$\frac{1}{2} \leq p_2 \quad \text{and} \quad p_1 < \frac{p_2^2}{1 - 2p_2 + 2p_2^2},$$

a simply majority is better;
ii) if not so, $\forall\ c_1 > c_1^\star$ unanimity is better.

This result can be summarized as follows. If p_1, $p_2 > 1/2$, and they are not very far apart, then simple majority is better. Otherwise, if the error cost is sufficiently high, unanimity is preferable. Some further insight may be gained through the following Fig. 1. On the abscissas we measure p_2, and on the ordinates the indifference value $c_1^\star$. The curves denoted by "pi", $i = 2, 3, \ldots, 9$, give $c_1^\star$ as a function of p_2 for $p_1 = 0.i$. The curves denoted by "di", $i = 1, 2, \ldots, 5$, represent $c_1^\star$ as a function of p_2 for $p_1 - p_2 = 0.i$. Recalling that the $\{p_i\}$ are a measure of individual skills and that $(p_1 - p_2)$ is the measure of the strength of the leadership, we may conclude that

i) for a given level of leadership, c_1^* is an increasing function of p_1;
ii) for a given p_1, c_1^* is a decreasing function of the leadership level.

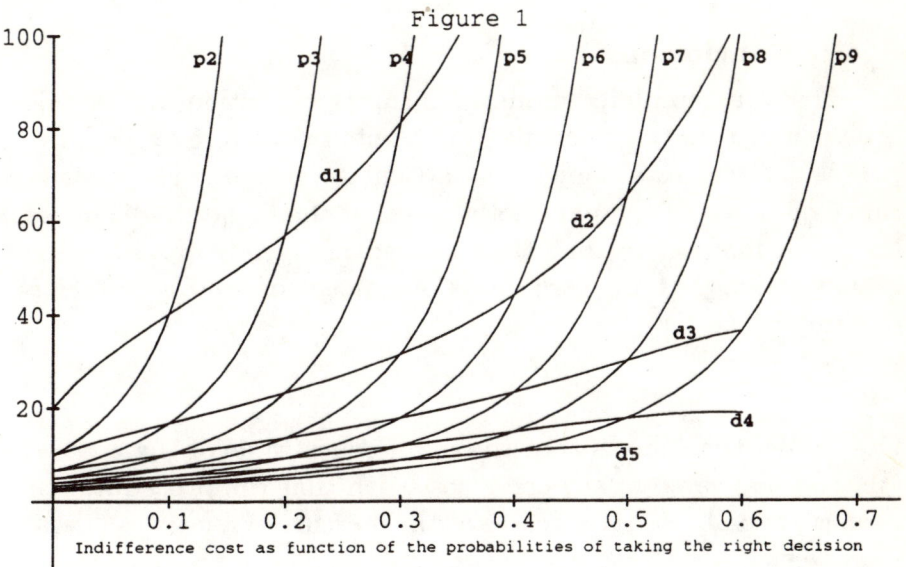

Figure 1

Indifference cost as function of the probabilities of taking the right decision

Now let us consider the unconventional case. We have

$$\gamma_1 = c_1(1 - p_1),$$
$$\gamma_2 = c_1(1 - p_2)(1 + p_2 - 2p_1 p_2) + \beta,$$

where β is the cost due to the collapse of the existing committee. Let $\hat{c}_1$ be the new indifference cost. Recalling that $p_1 < p_2$, by the same reasoning followed for conventional project above, we get the following result:

i) if

$$p_2 \leq \frac{1}{2} \quad \text{and} \quad p_1 > \frac{p_2^2}{1 - 2p_2 + 2p_2^2}$$

unanimity is better;

ii) otherwise, $\forall c_1 > \hat{c}_1$ simple majority is better.

In summary, if $p_1, p_2 \leq 1/2$, and they are not very far apart, then unanimity is always better. Otherwise, when the error is sufficiently high, simple majority is preferable.

4. Conclusions

Our very simplified model confirms the intuition that decisions over relevant matters benefit from slanted procedures.

What we have shown in particular (except for a restricted range of values of the parameters) is that the higher the *error cost*, the more likely it is that the most advantageous procedural rule is unanimity. Let us introduce the concept of *relative leadership*, measured by

$$\frac{p_1 - p_2}{p_1}.$$

Our model then shows that the indifference value of the *error cost* (that is, the value of the error cost such that the procedural rules perform equally well) decreases as the measure of relative leadership increases.

The intuition underlying the main results for the conventional case of this Chapter is that, given the particular composition of the decision structure (the characteristics and role of leadership), the unanimity rule gives power to the most skillful member, and therefore increases the probability of making the right decision. When the cost of making the wrong decision is sufficiently high, unanimity is therefore better.

In the unconventional case the results are essentially reversed. The simple majority rule gives more power to the younger members of the committee, who are the most skillful in this case, thereby increasing the probability of making the right decision. Consequently, if the cost related to the collapse of the existing decision structure is sufficiently high, the simple majority rule turns out to be most advantageous.

Appendix

We herein analyze in detail the conventional case, considering a board with three managers. When a project is scrutinized we initially have the following outcomes:

$$
\begin{array}{ccc}
A & A & A \\
A & A & R \\
A & R & A \\
A & R & R \\
R & A & A \\
R & A & R \\
R & R & A \\
R & R & R
\end{array}
$$

where A stands for acceptance of the project and R for its rejection. In each triple the first letter denotes the decision of the manager possessing the highest degree of skills while the remaining two letters denote the decision of the other two (homogeneous) managers. We may call each outcome a *state*. As described in the Introduction, the first manager is labelled with $i = 1$ and the other two with $i = 2, 3,$. p_i is the probability that the i-th manager accepts a good project, while q_i is the probability of accepting a bad project. Initially each member decides independently. Moreover,

$$p_1 > p_2 = p_3,$$

$$q_1 < q_2 = q_3.$$

Depending on the project being good or bad we get an *initial distribution* $\mathbf{p}_G$ or $\mathbf{p}_B$ which we write in vector form (each vector is a column vector):

$$\mathbf{p}_G = [p_1 p_2^2,\ p_1 p_2(1-p_2),\ p_1 p_2(1-p_2),\ p_1(1-p_2)^2,\ (1-p_1)p_2^2,$$
$$(1-p_1)p_2(1-p_2),\ (1-p_1)p_2(1-p_2),\ (1-p_1)(1-p_2)^2]',$$

$$\mathbf{p}_B = [q_1 q_2^2,\ q_1 q_2(1-q_2),\ q_1 q_2(1-q_2),\ q_1(1-q_2)^2,\ (1-q_1)q_2^2,$$
$$(1-q_1)q_2(1-q_2),\ (1-q_1)q_2(1-q_2),\ (1-q_1)(1-q_2)^2]',$$

The i-th entry in these vectors corresponds to the probability of the i-th state in the ordering given above.

If the board is initially split, the process through which unanimity is reached can be described by means of a Markov Chain, with the following assumptions.

1) Manager "1" is able to influence the other managers, yet is not influenced by them;

2) Managers "2" and "3" have a probability φ to maintain their initial decision, and they act independently of each other.

The transition matrix $\mathbf{Q}$ has the following form:

$$\mathbf{Q} = \begin{bmatrix} 1 & \mathbf{0} & 0 \\ \mathbf{u} & \mathbf{W} & \mathbf{v} \\ 0 & \mathbf{0} & 1 \end{bmatrix}.$$

where $\mathbf{u}$ is (6×1), $\mathbf{W}$ is (6×6), and $\mathbf{v}$ is (6×1). Moreover, $\mathbf{W}$ can be written as

$$\mathbf{W} = \begin{bmatrix} \mathbf{A} & \mathbf{0} \\ \mathbf{0} & \mathbf{EAE} \end{bmatrix},$$

where each submatrix is (3×3), $\mathbf{A}$ is given by

$$\mathbf{A} = \begin{bmatrix} \varphi^2 & (1-\varphi)^2 & \varphi(1-\varphi) \\ (1-\varphi)^2 & \varphi^2 & \varphi(1-\varphi) \\ \varphi(1-\varphi) & \varphi(1-\varphi) & \varphi^2 \end{bmatrix},$$

and $\mathbf{E}$ is the orthogonal matrix

$$\mathbf{E} = \begin{bmatrix} 0 & 0 & 1 \\ 0 & 1 & 0 \\ 1 & 0 & 0 \end{bmatrix}.$$

$\mathbf{u}$ and $\mathbf{v}$ can be written as

$$\mathbf{u} = \begin{bmatrix} \mathbf{u}_1 \\ \mathbf{0} \end{bmatrix}, \quad \mathbf{v} = \begin{bmatrix} \mathbf{0} \\ \mathbf{v}_1 \end{bmatrix},$$

where each subvector is (3×1) and

$$\mathbf{u}_1 = \begin{bmatrix} \varphi(1-\varphi) \\ \varphi(1-\varphi) \\ (1-\varphi)^2 \end{bmatrix}, \quad \mathbf{v}_1 = \begin{bmatrix} (1-\varphi)^2 \\ \varphi(1-\varphi) \\ \varphi(1-\varphi) \end{bmatrix}.$$

Because $\mathbf{Q}$ is a transition matrix, we have

$$\mathbf{u} + \mathbf{v} + \mathbf{W}\mathbf{e}_6 = \mathbf{e}_6,$$

and so

$$\mathbf{u} + \mathbf{v} = (\mathbf{I} - \mathbf{W})\mathbf{e}_6,$$

where $\mathbf{I}$ is the identity matrix and $\mathbf{e}_6$ is a (6×1)-vector of all ones. Considering the block structure of $\mathbf{W}$, we have the simplified relationships

$$\mathbf{u}_1 + \mathbf{A}\mathbf{e}_3 = \mathbf{e}_3,$$

which implies

$$\mathbf{u}_1 = (\mathbf{I} - \mathbf{A})\mathbf{e}_3,$$

and

$$\mathbf{v}_1 + \mathbf{E}\mathbf{A}\mathbf{E}\mathbf{e}_3 = \mathbf{e}_3,$$

which implies

$$\mathbf{v}_1 = \mathbf{E}(\mathbf{I} - \mathbf{A})\mathbf{E}\mathbf{e}_3.$$

Let τ_G and τ_B be the times required to reach unanimity if the project is good or bad, respectively.
Then

$$Pr[\tau_J = 0] = \mathbf{p}'_J \mathbf{r},$$
$$Pr[\tau_J = k] = \mathbf{p}'_J (\mathbf{Q}^k - \mathbf{Q}^{k-1})\mathbf{r},$$

where J stands for G or B, and $\mathbf{r}$ is a (8×1)-vector with the first and the 8-th elements equal to 1 and the remaining equal to 0.
This is a proper distribution if $\lim_{i \to \infty} \mathbf{Q}^i$ exists and it is equal to (say) $\mathbf{Q}^\infty$.
Since

$$\mathbf{Q}^i = \begin{bmatrix} 1 & \mathbf{0} & 0 \\ \sum_{h=0}^{i-1} \mathbf{W}^h \mathbf{u} & \mathbf{W}^i & \sum_{h=0}^{i-1} \mathbf{W}^h \mathbf{v} \\ 0 & \mathbf{0} & 1 \end{bmatrix},$$

this amounts to ascertaining whether all the eigenvalues of $\mathbf{W}$ are, in absolute value, strictly less than 1.
Given the structure of $\mathbf{W}$, this in turn implies studying the spectrum of $\mathbf{A}$. Given our assumptions about φ, a result by Catalani

(1993) allows us to conclude that all the eigenvalues of $\mathbf{W}$ are indeed, in absolute value, strictly less than 1.
Now

$$\mathbf{Q}^k - \mathbf{Q}^{k-1} = \begin{bmatrix} 0 & \mathbf{0} & 0 \\ \mathbf{W}^{k-1}\mathbf{u} & \mathbf{W}^{k-1}(\mathbf{W}-\mathbf{I}) & \mathbf{W}^{k-1}\mathbf{v} \\ 0 & \mathbf{0} & 0 \end{bmatrix},$$

and so the expected value of the transition time τ_J is given by

$$\mathbf{E}[\tau_J] = \mathbf{p}'_J \sum_{k=1}^{\infty} k(\mathbf{Q}^k - \mathbf{Q}^{k-1})\mathbf{r},$$

where

$$\sum_{k=1}^{\infty} k(\mathbf{Q}^k - \mathbf{Q}^{k-1}) =$$

$$= \begin{bmatrix} 0 & \mathbf{0} & 0 \\ \sum_{k=1}^{\infty} k\mathbf{W}^{k-1}\mathbf{u} & \sum_{k=1}^{\infty} k\mathbf{W}^{k-1}(\mathbf{W}-\mathbf{I}) & \sum_{k=1}^{\infty} k\mathbf{W}^{k-1}\mathbf{v} \\ 0 & \mathbf{0} & 0 \end{bmatrix}.$$

We know that the power series

$$\sum_{p=0}^{\infty} \lambda^p$$

converges to

$$f(\lambda) = \frac{1}{1-\lambda}$$

for

$$|\lambda| < 1,$$

and so it may be differentiated term by term any number of times within the circle of convergence. Consequently

$$\sum_{p=1}^{\infty} p\lambda^{p-1} = \frac{1}{(1-\lambda)^2}.$$

Using results in matrix theory (see Gantmacher (1974)), we know that this expansion remains valid when the scalar argument λ is replaced by a matrix whose eigenvalues lie within the circle of convergence.
This being the case for $\mathbf{W}$, we get

$$\sum_{k=1}^{\infty} k \mathbf{W}^{k-1} = (\mathbf{I} - \mathbf{W})^{-2},$$

and consequently

$$\sum_{k=1}^{\infty} k(\mathbf{Q}^k - \mathbf{Q}^{k-1})\mathbf{r} = \begin{bmatrix} 0 \\ (\mathbf{I} - \mathbf{W})^{-2}(\mathbf{u} + \mathbf{v}) \\ 0 \end{bmatrix}.$$

Finally, writing π_{J1} and π_{J2} for the (3×1)-vectors made up, respectively, by the 2-nd, 3-rd, 4-th element and the 5-th, 6-th, 7-th element of $\mathbf{p}_J$, we get

$$E[\tau_J] = \pi'_{J1}(\mathbf{I} - \mathbf{A})^{-1}\mathbf{e}_3 + \pi'_{J2}E(\mathbf{I} - \mathbf{A})^{-1}\mathbf{E}\mathbf{e}_3.$$

What is the probability that the project be accepted with unanimity? Intuitively, it is p_1 if the project is good, and q_1 if the project is bad. That it is indeed so is confirmed by the fact that

$$Pr[A|\text{the project is good}] = \mathbf{p}'_G \mathbf{Q}^\infty \mathbf{r}_1,$$

where $\mathbf{r}_1$ is a (8×1)-vector with the first element equal to one and all the others equal to zero. Then

$$\begin{aligned} \mathbf{p}'_G \mathbf{Q}^\infty \mathbf{r}_1 &= p_1 p_2^2 + \pi'_{G1}(\mathbf{I} - \mathbf{A})^{-1}\mathbf{u}_1 \\ &= p_1 p_2^2 + \pi'_{G1}\mathbf{e}_3 \\ &= p_1. \end{aligned}$$

Analogously it is proved that

$$\begin{aligned} Pr[A|\text{the project is bad}] &= \mathbf{p}'_B \mathbf{Q}^\infty \mathbf{r}_2 \\ &= q_1, \end{aligned}$$

where
$$r_1 + r_2 = r.$$

In what follows we confine ourselves to the case when the scrutinized project is good.

It seems reasonable to measure the strength of the leadership by the quantity $p_1 - p_2$, so
$$\varphi = 1 - (p_1 - p_2).$$

Simple calculation shows that
$$\mathbf{E}[\tau_G] = \frac{p_2(1-p_2) + 2(1-p_1+p_2)(p_1+p_2-2p_1p_2)}{(p_1-p_2)(1-p_1+p_2)}.$$

If c_1 is the cost incurred by rejecting a good project, then the total average cost incurred by a structure ruled by unanimity is
$$\gamma_1 = \mathbf{E}[\tau_G] + c_1 \mathbf{Pr}[R|\text{the project is good}]$$
$$= \mathbf{E}[\tau_G] + c_1(1-p_1),$$

that is, the cost related to the time spent in reaching unanimity plus the average cost of the outcome of the made decision.

Considering the table of states given at the beginning of this Appendix, we see that, after simplifying, the total average cost incurred by a structure ruled by simple majority is
$$\gamma_2 = c_1(1-p_2)(1+p_2-2p_1p_2).$$

Our key variable is the
$$\Delta = \gamma_1 - \gamma_2$$
$$= c_1[(1-p_1) - (1-p_2)(1+p_2-2p_1p_2)] + \mathbf{E}[\tau_G].$$

$\Delta < 0$ means that unanimity is superior.

Let us set $\Delta = 0$ and solve the resulting equation for c_1. Let $c_1^\star$ denote the solution; then $c_1^\star$ is the indifference cost:
$$c_1^\star = \frac{-\mathbf{E}[\tau_G]}{[(1-p_1) - (1-p_2)(1+p_2-2p_1p_2)]}.$$

Given that $\mathbf{E}[\tau_G] > 0$, to have $c_1^* \geq 0$ (which means a meaningful solution) it is necessary that

$$(1 - p_1) - (1 - p_2)(1 + p_2 - 2p_1 p_2) < 0. \qquad (\star)$$

Otherwise, simple majority is always superior.
Since in the conventional case $p_1 > p_2$, we see that if $p_1 \leq 1/2$, then the above inequality $(\star)$ always holds.
Aside from this case, the inequality $(\star)$ holds if

$$p_1 > \frac{p_2^2}{1 - 2p_2 + 2p_2^2}.$$

So in this situation for all $c_1 > c_1^*$ unanimity is better. On the other hand, if

$$p_2 < p_1 < \frac{p_2^2}{1 - 2p_2 + 2p_2^2},$$

which implies

$$\frac{1}{2} \leq p_2 < 1,$$

whatever c_1, then simple majority always performs better.
The dependence of the solution c_1^* on the parameters p_1 and p_2 is a troublesome problem. The best way to deal with it is to focus on the picture given in Section 4.

CHAPTER II

MAJORITY RULES AND EFFICIENCY OF THE DECISION PROCESS

1. Introduction

Daily experience in different fields shows that in the case of dichotomous decisions, the consequences of which might be particularly important, the decision body normally does not choose according to a simple majority, but according to a special (qualified) majority, or unanimity. For example, Democratic Parliaments act mostly according to a qualified majority in the case of amendments of the Constitutional Chart, as does the Board of Directors of a corporation when deciding on strategic matters such as mergers, changes of the charter and so on.

We know of no formal model justifying such a constraint, and generally, evidence for it is accepted without explanation. For instance, "it makes sense to slant the decision procedure ... a good corporate example may be the imposition of a significant special majority requirement in cases of 'important' decisions, such as mergers, liquidations, or charter amendments." (Nitzan and Procaccia, 1986, p.198).

We presume the following about possible motivations for this situation:

(a) the desire for a maximum involvement of all the members of the decision body,
(b) the feeling that the probability to make the correct decision increases with the number of members who agree on it.

While we are not going to analyse point (a), it is worthwhile to consider that a deeper involvement might strengthen the identification of each member with the whole decision body. This would counteract any tendency toward selfish interest detrimental to that pertaining to the decision body.

In this chapter we present a model to assess whether and when it is advantageous to give up the simple majority in favour of a qualified one. First we shall define the meaning of advantageous in our context. Facing a dichotomous choice we will incur a positive payoff π in the case of a correct decision and a negative payoff (cost) γ in the case of a wrong decision. Without loss of generality we can assume $\pi = 0$. Beside this cost γ we now introduce another type of cost δ, which is the cost relative to the time required to reach the decision according to the required majority. To model this situation let us assume that the number of members n be odd; with a simple majority we will set $\delta = 0$. Otherwise, in the case of a qualified majority we shall see there is a positive probability that the decision body not reach the required majority. It will then be necessary to reconvene the decision body, and perhaps to reconvene it again, and so on, up to the point at which the required majority is reached. In such a case we will let $\delta > 0$, increasing with the number of meetings of the decision body. Therefore the expected total cost of the decision process can be divided in two components: the expected cost related to the correctness of the taken decision, and the cost of the expected time spent to reach the decision. In our context, we define as advantageous the decision rule which minimises the expected total cost. We would like to stress that this analysis in terms of advantage produces results analogous to those obtained in Chapter I of Part I. In Section 3 a more detailed comparison of the two models is offered.

2. The model

Let us consider a decision body composed of n members whose duty it is to make a dichotomous choice. These members share the same goal and the same probability p to make the correct decision. Each member acts independently of the others. As we said in Section 1, the wrong decision entails a cost γ. We will analyse different majority rules, going from the simple majority to unanimity. For convenience we will let n be odd. Let us denote with k the required majority. In the case of simple majority $k = k^\star = (n+1)/2$, and in the case of unanimity $k = n$.

If $k > k^\star$ it is evident that the decision body might not reach the required majority and consequently the decision. In contrast, in the case of a simple majority a decision is always reached. Let us denote with C_k the event that the decision body, ruled by a majority k, makes the correct decision, with A_k the event that at least k members of the decision body make the correct decision, with B_k the event that at least k members take the wrong decision. So $C_k = A_k$. Now let R_k be the event that the decision body has reached the required majority. Then for each $k \geq k^\star$:

$$R_k = A_k \cup B_k. \tag{1}$$

A key note of our model is given by

$$\mathcal{P}_k = \mathbf{Pr}[C_k|R_k] = \mathbf{Pr}[A_k|R_k], \tag{2}$$

that is, the probability that the decision body make the correct decision, given that the required majority has been reached. Clearly

$$\mathbf{Pr}[C_{k^\star}|R_{k^\star}] = \mathbf{Pr}[C_{k^\star}] = \mathbf{Pr}[A_{k^\star}]. \tag{3}$$

One can see that

$$\mathbf{Pr}[C_k|R_k] = \frac{\mathbf{Pr}[A_k]}{\mathbf{Pr}[A_k] + \mathbf{Pr}[B_k]}, \qquad k > k^\star. \tag{4}$$

In the Appendix we show that for $p > 1/2$ the quantity $\mathcal{P}_k$ increases uniformly with $k \geq k^\star$. For $p < 1/2$ we have the opposite result, while for $p = 1/2$ the quantity $\mathcal{P}_k$ remains constant. Let us note that if $p > 1/2$, then always $\mathcal{P}_k > p$, that is the performance of the decision body is always better than that of its members (and the opposite is true if $p < 1/2$). This can be considered as an extension of Condorcet's jury theorem (Berg, 1993a, 1993b, 1994).

Now if $k > k^\star$ there is a positive probability, given by $1 - \mathbf{Pr}[R_k]$, that the decision body does not reach the required majority. In such a case a second reconvening is necessary, and perhaps a third and so on, up to the point at which the required majority is reached. This sequence of reconvenings implies a cost due to delay, which can be considered a transaction cost. Let us denote with π the positive payoff associated with a right decision with π and the negative payoff in the case of a wrong decision with γ. To this cost we must add another cost δ_k associated with the delay. δ_k is an increasing function of k, and for $k = k^\star$ we have $\delta = 0$.

For convenience, but without loss of generality, we set $\pi = 0$ and $\gamma = 1$; so the interesting problem is to assess the expected total cost as a function of the rule k. We can model δ_k as follows

$$\delta_k = d \cdot \mathbf{E}[\tau_k], \qquad (5)$$

where $d \geq 0$ is a constant, $\mathbf{E}[\tau_k]$ is the expected waiting time of the attainment of the required majority. It follows that

$$\mathbf{E}[\tau_k] = \frac{1}{\mathbf{Pr}[A_k] + \mathbf{Pr}[B_k]} - 1, \qquad (6)$$

and then the expected total cost EC_k can be written as

$$EC_k = \frac{\mathbf{Pr}[B_k]}{\mathbf{Pr}[A_k] + \mathbf{Pr}[B_k]} + d \left[\frac{1}{\mathbf{Pr}[A_k] + \mathbf{Pr}[B_k]} - 1 \right]. \qquad (7)$$

Since

$$\frac{\mathbf{Pr}[B_k]}{\mathbf{Pr}[A_k] + \mathbf{Pr}[B_k]} = 1 - \mathcal{P}_k,$$

it follows from the above considerations that if $p \leq 1/2$ then the minimum EC_k is attained uniformly for $k = k^\star$. The case $p > 1/2$ is more complex. Let $d = 0$. Then

$$EC_k = 1 - \mathcal{P}_k, \qquad (8)$$

and since $\mathcal{P}_k$ increases uniformly with k we can conclude that EC_k decreases uniformly as k increases: the minimum will be attained at $k = n$, that is with unanimity. On the contrary, if $d = 1$, we have

$$EC_k = \frac{1 - \mathbf{Pr}[A_k]}{\mathbf{Pr}[A_k] + \mathbf{Pr}[B_k]}. \tag{9}$$

From (9) it follows that as k increases, the numerator increases and the denominator decreases. Therefore EC_k increases uniformly with k and the minimum will be reached when $k = k^*$. *A fortiori* setting $d = 1 + \varepsilon$, $\varepsilon > 0$, we can see that the expected total cost is uniformly minimum for $k = k^*$. So now we turn to the case $0 < d < 1$. Since we set $\gamma = 1$, this is equivalent to considering the transaction cost as a fraction of the decision cost.

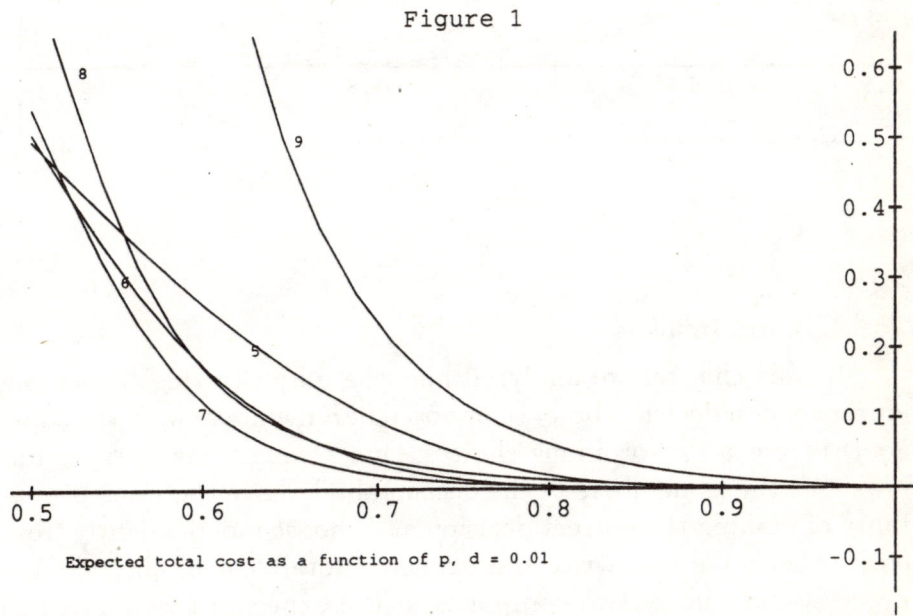

Figure 1

Expected total cost as a function of p, d = 0.01

When $0 < d < 1$ there is no majority rule which uniformly performs better. The following three figures graph EC_k as a function of p, $p > 1/2$. In all the figures we set $n = 9$. The values of d are $d = 0.01, d = 0.005, d = 0.001$, respectively. The numbers marking each curve denote the values of k: $5 \leq k \leq 9$. We see that as d approaches 0, the most advantageous rules, while not uniformly, are to be found among those with $k > k^*$. Only for values of p approaching 0 does the simple majority remain competitive.

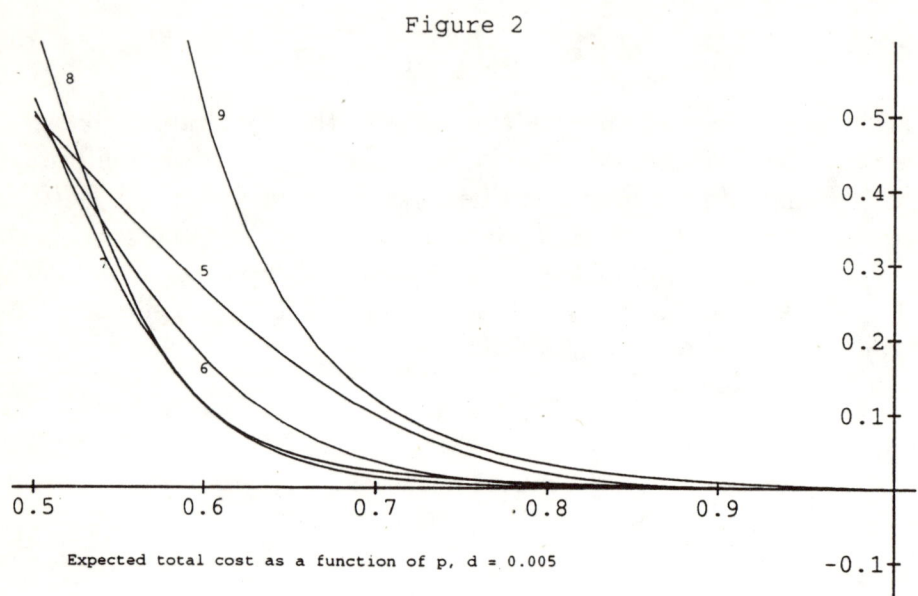

Figure 2

Expected total cost as a function of p, d = 0.005

3. Conclusions

In this chapter we analysed how the majority rules affect the efficiency of a decision body (composed of n members with the same goal) facing a dichotomous choice. Our assumptions were as follows. All the n members of the decision body have the same probability of making the correct decision and choose independently from each other. We can write the expected total cost of the decision process as a sum of two components: the expected cost related to the correctness of the taken decision and the cost of the expected time necessary to reach the decision. We define as advantageous the majority rule that minimizes the expected total cost. In Chapter I of Part I we built another model to study the same problem. The assumptions were as follows. All the members, but one, of the decision body are homogeneous with respect to their skills and make decisions independently one from each other. The one possessing greater skills acts as a leader and affects the decision of the other members. In both models the majority rules with $k > k^*$ entail a cost due to the delay in reaching the decision which is an increasing function of the delay. In the present paper we model the delay through a random variable describing the time necessary to reach the required majority. In the first model we examined by means of a stochastic process how some members change their initial opinion under the influence of the leader, until the required majority is eventually reached. The behaviour of the members affected by the leader is described by a Markov Chain. Summarizing, both models show that the determination of the most advantageous majority rule rests on the ratio between the cost due to the delay and the cost associated with the wrong decision. The advantage of more stringent majority rules increases when the above ratio decreases. In our former model the strength of leadership is a factor which reduces the cost due to delay.

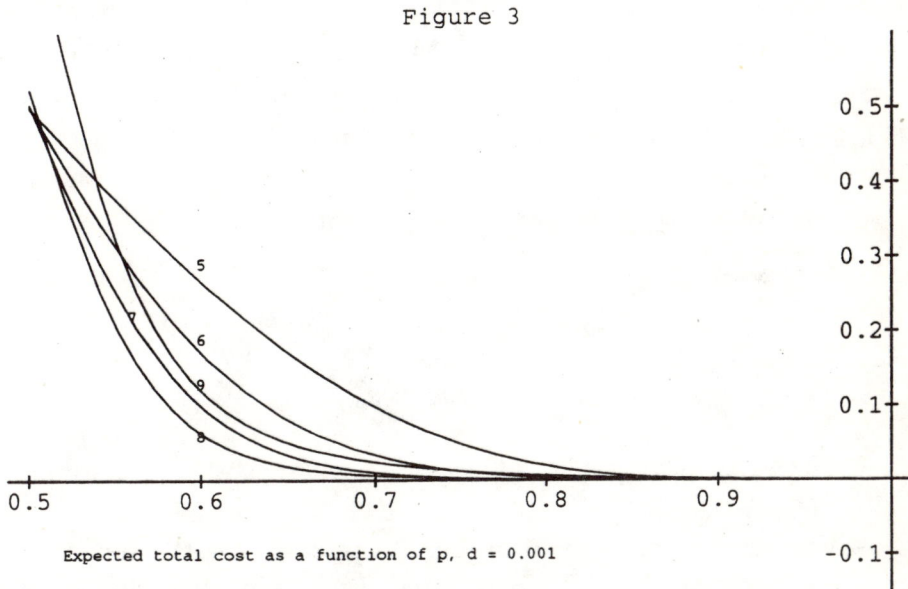

Figure 3

Expected total cost as a function of p, d = 0.001

The problem dealt with in this paper belongs to the economic literature which Sah and Stiglitz (1986, 1988a, 1988b) referred to as "the architecture of the economic systems". More particularly, this chapter is akin to their research on the determination of the optimal consensus level in a committee composed of n members. We share the same initial assumptions, although we do not differentiate between Type I and Type II errors. Furthermore we explicitly introduce the cost due to the likely delay incurred when the required majority is more stringent than the simple one.

Appendix

In this Appendix we will show that, when $p > 1/2$, the quantity $\mathcal{P}_k$ increases uniformly with $k \geq k^*$. For $p < 1/2$ the opposite result holds, while for $p = 1/2$ the quantity $\mathcal{P}_k$ is constant. Let $p > 1/2$. We have

$$\mathbf{Pr}[A_k] = \sum_{i=k}^{n} \binom{n}{i} p^i (1-p)^{n-i},$$

$$\mathbf{Pr}[B_k] = \sum_{i=0}^{n-k} \binom{n}{i} p^i (1-p)^{n-i}.$$

Consequently

$$\mathbf{Pr}[A_{k+1}] = \mathbf{Pr}[A_k] - \binom{n}{k} p^k (1-p)^{n-k},$$

$$\mathbf{Pr}[B_{k+1}] = \mathbf{Pr}[B_k] - \binom{n}{n-k} p^{n-k} (1-p)^k,$$

$$\mathbf{Pr}[A_{k+1}] + \mathbf{Pr}[B_{k+1}] =$$
$$= \mathbf{Pr}[A_k] + \mathbf{Pr}[B_k] - \binom{n}{k} \left[p^k (1-p)^{n-k} + p^{n-k} (1-p)^k \right].$$

Now consider $\mathcal{P}_k$ as defined in (2). It appears that the numerator in the expression for $\mathcal{P}_{k+1}$ is reduced, with respect to that of $\mathcal{P}_k$, by the amount $\binom{n}{k} p^k (1-p)^{n-k}$, while the denominator is reduced by the amount

$$\binom{n}{k} \left[p^k (1-p)^{n-k} + p^{n-k} (1-p)^k \right].$$

Let us consider that, if all the quantities that appear are positive, then
$$\frac{a-x}{b-y} > \frac{a}{b} \quad \text{if} \quad \frac{b}{a} < \frac{y}{x}. \qquad (\star)$$

Setting $a = \mathbf{Pr}[A_k]$, $b = \mathbf{Pr}[A_k] + \mathbf{Pr}[B_k]$, the result is
$$\frac{b}{a} = 1 + \frac{\mathbf{Pr}[B_k]}{\mathbf{Pr}[A_k]}.$$

On the other hand
$$\frac{y}{x} = 1 + \frac{p^{n-k}(1-p)^k}{p^k(1-p)^{n-k}}$$
$$= 1 + p^{n-2k}(1-p)^{2k-n}$$
$$= 1 + \left(\frac{p}{1-p}\right)^{n-2k}.$$

Now, if $p > 1/2$, we have $\frac{p}{1-p} > 1$, while $\mathbf{Pr}[B_k] < \mathbf{Pr}[A_k]$, since for these values of p the right tail of the binomial distribution is heavier than the left one and the elementary elements composing B_k e A_k are symmetrical with respect to $n/2$. Comparing the last two equations we can conclude that
$$\frac{y}{x} > \frac{b}{a},$$
and thus, using $(\star)$, we have
$$\mathcal{P}_{k+1} > \mathcal{P}_k, \quad k \geq k^\star, \quad p > \frac{1}{2}.$$

The same reasoning, with necessary modifications, proves that, if $p < 1/2$, then $\mathcal{P}_k$ decreases inversely with k.

CHAPTER III

TEAM COOPERATION VS. INDEPENDENT ASSESSMENT †

If the dictator knew everything there was to know about every problem she faced, there would seem to be no self-interested reason to create an independent (and therefore potentially competitive) force. But without omniscience, omnipotence might be dangerous (G.J. Miller, 1992).

Two relatively independent heads are better than two relatively dependent heads (J. Bendor, 1985).

1. Introduction

The essential goal of this chapter is to analyse the following situation: provided that someone (an entrepreneur, a dictator and so on) decides to ask someone else for advice in order to reach

---

† Reprinted, with slight modifications, from *Riv. Inter. di Scienze Economiche e Commerciali*, 2, 1993.

a correct decision, should she organise a decision structure that acts cooperatively or independently? For example, an entrepreneur might decide to resort to such a kind of decision structure either because of her information asymmetry or because of lack of skills.

We assume the following.

1. Human decisions are subject to errors.

2. Information gathering and processing are a substantial and expensive part of the decision process.

3. The nature of the decision errors depends on the characteristics of the decision organization.

The economic literature (Sah, 1991; Sah and Stiglitz, 1985, 1986, 1988 3a 1, 1988 3b 1, 1991; Koh, 1992; Bull and Ordover, 1987) on this topic has traditionally assumed that every member of any decision organization is identical and independent in the decision making process.

Given these hypotheses it is possible to differentiate and compare decision structures of any organization whose goal it is to maximize performance (measured for example by expected profit). By changing some parameters (for example, the quality of the project portfolio, the number of members of the structure, the skills of the members, the level of consensus) it is also possible to ascertain how we can improve the performance of the organization. This hypothesis of independence is not so cogent in some formal models concerning the jury decision process (Klevorick and Rothschild, 1979; Klevorick and others, 1984), where some form of cooperation is implicitly assumed in the deliberation process.

Our way of modelling the cooperation of a decision structure rests on the introduction of a particular member, the *leader*, who for our purposes is characterized by the fact that his decision influences the decisions made by the other members of the organization.

We present the following situation in our model. An advertising firm must develop a good idea concerning the best way to advertise a new product. The firm owner has some collaborators, and is faced with the dilemma of having them work together (cooperatively) or independently. In which case are they more likely to come up with a good idea?

2. The model

In our model "good idea" refers to the capability of distinguishing between a good and a bad project. More precisely we assume that "good idea" means accepting a good project.

The firm owner has n collaborators. Let's assume that each them has the same probability of developing a good idea, called probability p. We assume that if the collaborators work together, one of them will emerge as leader. Furthermore if they are working cooperatively, the leader will influence the other collaborators, who are otherwise independent in their decision process. We model this influence as follows. Given that the leader has accepted a good project, the probability that any other collaborator will accept it is $\bar{p} > p$. Obviously if the n collaborators work independently, the role of the leader disappears.

We are now mainly concerned with comparing the performance of these two decision structures (cooperation versus independence) in terms of the probability of accepting a good project. From another point of view we can characterize our model by saying that the members of the decision structure commit only type I errors (e.g. rejection of good projects). Our structures decide according to a given consensus level k with $1 \leq k \leq n$: the structure accepts the (good) project if at least k members accept it. Let us denote with $\mathcal{P}^T_{n,k}$ the probability that a team with n members and a consensus level of k chooses a (good) project. Analogously, let $\mathcal{P}^I_{n,k}$ be the probability of the same event in the case of independence.

Henceforth we are going to discuss qualitatively the main results obtained. The proofs will be given in the Appendix.

First of all it is easy to prove that if $k = 1$, then independence is always better than cooperation, for whatever the values of $p, \bar{p}, n$, that is

$$\mathcal{P}^T_{n,1} < \mathcal{P}^I_{n,1}.$$

The opposite result is obtained if $k = n$, that is, for whatever value of $p, \bar{p}, n$, cooperation is always better than independence:

$$\mathcal{P}^T_{n,n} > \mathcal{P}^I_{n,n}.$$

Furthermore, if n is odd and $k = (n+1)/2$, we have the following result:

$$\text{if} \quad p = \frac{1}{2}, \quad \text{then} \quad \mathcal{P}^T_{n,k} = \mathcal{P}^I_{n,k} = \frac{1}{2},$$

$$\text{if} \quad p < \frac{1}{2}, \quad \text{then} \quad \mathcal{P}^T_{n,k} > \mathcal{P}^I_{n,k},$$

$$\text{if} \quad p > \frac{1}{2}, \quad \text{then} \quad \mathcal{P}^T_{n,k} < \mathcal{P}^I_{n,k}.$$

For other values of k, consider the case $n = 5$. Numerical calculations for a grid of values of p show that:
for $k = 2$

$$\text{when} \quad p = 0.1 \qquad \mathcal{P}^T_{5,2} > \mathcal{P}^I_{5,2};$$

$$\text{when} \quad p = 0.2 \qquad 0.2 < \bar{p} < 0.4 \qquad \mathcal{P}^T_{5,2} < \mathcal{P}^I_{5,2},$$

$$\text{when} \quad p = 0.2 \qquad 0.4 < \bar{p} < 1.0 \qquad \mathcal{P}^T_{5,2} < \mathcal{P}^I_{5,2};$$

for values of p greater than 0.3:

$$\mathcal{P}^T_{5,2} < \mathcal{P}^I_{5,2}.$$

As for $k = 4$

$$\text{when} \quad p < 0.8 \qquad \mathcal{P}^T_{5,4} > \mathcal{P}^I_{5,4};$$

$$\text{when} \quad p = 0.8 \qquad 0.8 < \bar{p} < 0.85 \qquad \mathcal{P}^T_{5,4} < \mathcal{P}^I_{5,4},$$

$$\text{when} \quad p = 0.8 \qquad 0.85 < \bar{p} < 1.0 \qquad \mathcal{P}^T_{5,4} > \mathcal{P}^I_{5,4},$$

$$\text{when} \quad p \geq 0.9 \qquad \mathcal{P}^T_{5,4} < \mathcal{P}^I_{5,4}.$$

It is possible to make the following qualitative generalizations. For any n, k and p it is possible to find a $p^\star$ such that

$$\text{if} \quad 0 < p < \bar{p} < p^\star, \quad \text{then} \quad \mathcal{P}^T > \mathcal{P}^I,$$

$$\text{if} \quad p < p^\star < \bar{p} < 1, \quad \text{then} \quad \mathcal{P}^T < \mathcal{P}^I.$$

What happens is that, for a given n,

$$\text{if} \quad k \to 1, \quad p^\star \to 0,$$

$$\text{if} \quad k \to n, \quad p^\star \to 1.$$

So far, the analysis has not dealt with the cost of the leader. Resorting to the services of a leader entails an additional cost. So for any given n and k in choosing between cooperation and independence the owner has to take into account not only the value of the probability of accepting a (good) project but also the additional cost of a leader.

The owner has the goal of maximizing the expected return resulting from the made decision. Let $z > 0$ be the benefit flow relative to a good project. As we stated in our model, the decision structure does not accept a bad project, while it can refuse a good project. If a good project is rejected, the owner suffers an opportunity cost equal to $-z$.

Furthermore let π denote the probability that the evaluated project be good. In this context the expected return $\mathcal{E}$ is given by:

a) in the case of independence

$$\mathcal{E}^I(n,\,k) = \pi z \mathcal{P}^I_{n,k} - \pi z (1 - \mathcal{P}^I_{n,k})$$
$$= 2\pi z \mathcal{P}^I_{n,k} - \pi z,$$

b) in the case of cooperation

$$\mathcal{E}^T(n,\,k) = 2\pi z \mathcal{P}^T_{n,k} - \pi z - w,$$

where w is the leader's wage, after setting to zero the wages of the other $n-1$ members, or, in other terms, the additional cost of the leader.

Let

$$\Delta(n\,k) = \mathcal{E}^T(n,\,k) - \mathcal{E}^I(n,\,k) \qquad (1)$$
$$= 2\pi z (\mathcal{P}^T_{n,k} - \mathcal{P}^I_{n,k}) - w.$$

The owner will choose between the independence and the cooperation form according to the sign of $\Delta(n,\,k)$. If $\Delta(n,\,k) > 0$ then cooperation is preferred; if $\Delta(n,\,k) < 0$ then independence will be chosen.

To attain $\Delta(n,\,k) > 0$ it is necessary that $\mathcal{P}^T_{n,k} - \mathcal{P}^I_{n,k} > 0$. To approach the solution to this problem we are going to confine ourselves to the case where n is odd and $k = (n+1)/2$, which can be called the *simple majority rule*.

As we have seen $\mathcal{P}^T_{n,k} - \mathcal{P}^I_{n,k} > 0$ only if $p < 1/2$. This is a necessary condition in order to prefer cooperation. So restricting ourselves to values of $p < 1/2$, the behavior of $\Delta(n, k) > 0$ depends on π, z and w.

Now we model the leadership which appears through the relationship between p and $\bar{p}$. The stronger is the leadership, the higher is the value of $\bar{p}$ with respect to p. One way to formalize this idea is to write

$$\bar{p} = \frac{m}{m+1} + \frac{p}{m+1}.$$

For $m \to 0$, $\bar{p} \to p$; for $m \to \infty$, $\bar{p} \to 1$.

So m is a parameter denoting the degree of the leadership (the charisma of the leader).

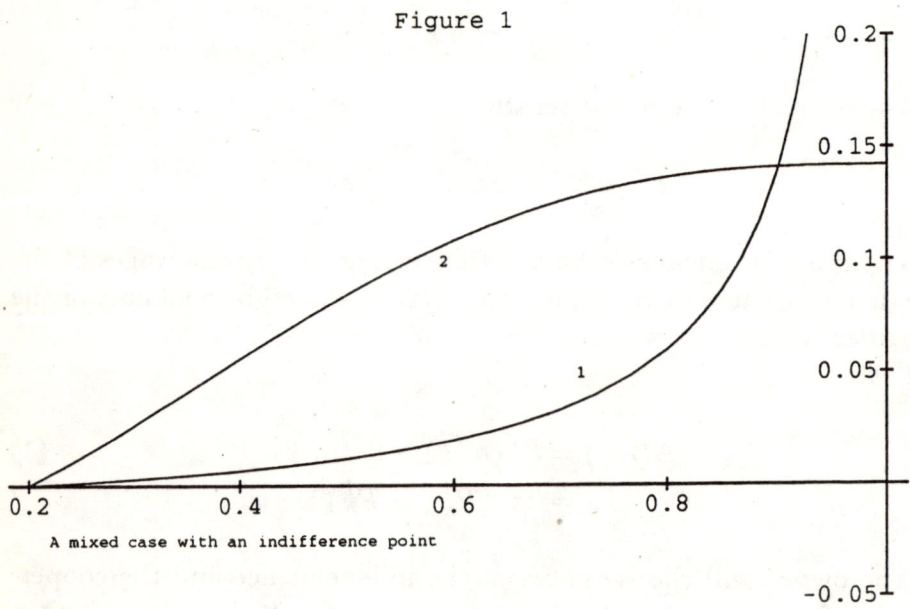

Figure 1

A mixed case with an indifference point

It seems reasonable to assume a positive correlation between w and m. The qualitative behavior of $\Delta(n, k)$ is not substantially influenced by the assumption $w = m$.

From equation (1) and assuming $\mathcal{P}^T_{n,k} - \mathcal{P}^I_{n,k} > 0$, it is clear that the preferability of cooperation increases with π and z, while it decreases with w.

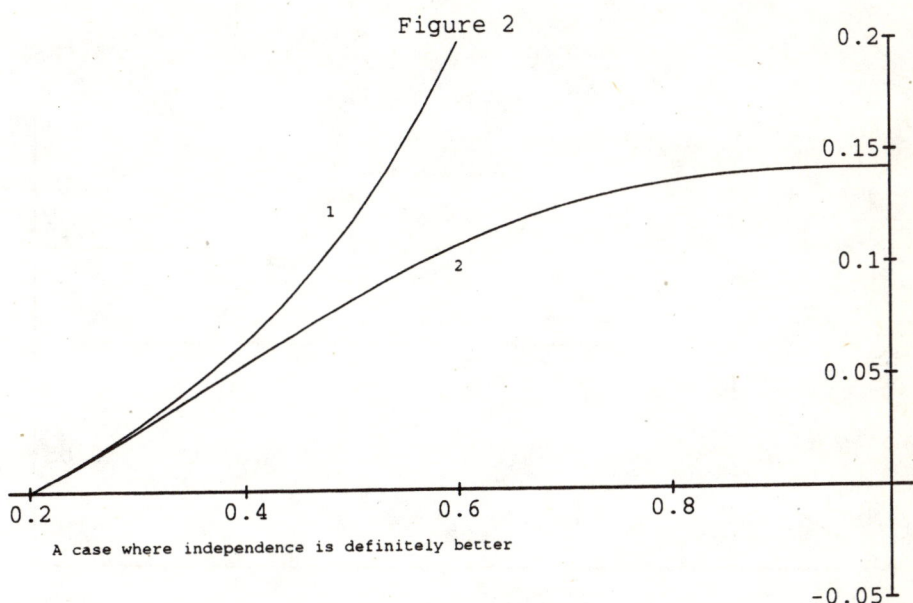

Figure 2

A case where independence is definitely better

To analyse the effect of p on Δ let us consider for example the case where $n = 5$. In the graphs we draw two curves (both as a function of $\overline{3p}$): curve 1 depicts $w/2\pi z$, curve 2 depicts $\mathcal{P}^T_{n,k} - \mathcal{P}^I_{n,k}$. Independence is preferred for any $\overline{p}$ such that curve 1 is greater than curve 2.

In the Appendix we derive a sufficient condition for independence being preferred:

$$z < \frac{1}{6\pi(1-p)^2(1-2p)}, \qquad p < \frac{1}{2}. \qquad (2)$$

If this inequality is satisfied then we are in the situation depicted in graph 2. The right hand side of the above inequality increases with p. So if we are in graph 2 we remain in the same graph *a fortiori*. On the other hand if we are in graph 1 we might move to graph 2, meaning that independence becomes more and more preferable as p increases.

Due to both logic and budget constraints, a threshold m_0 exists such that for every $m > m_0$, then $w = w_0$ (finite). See Figure 3.

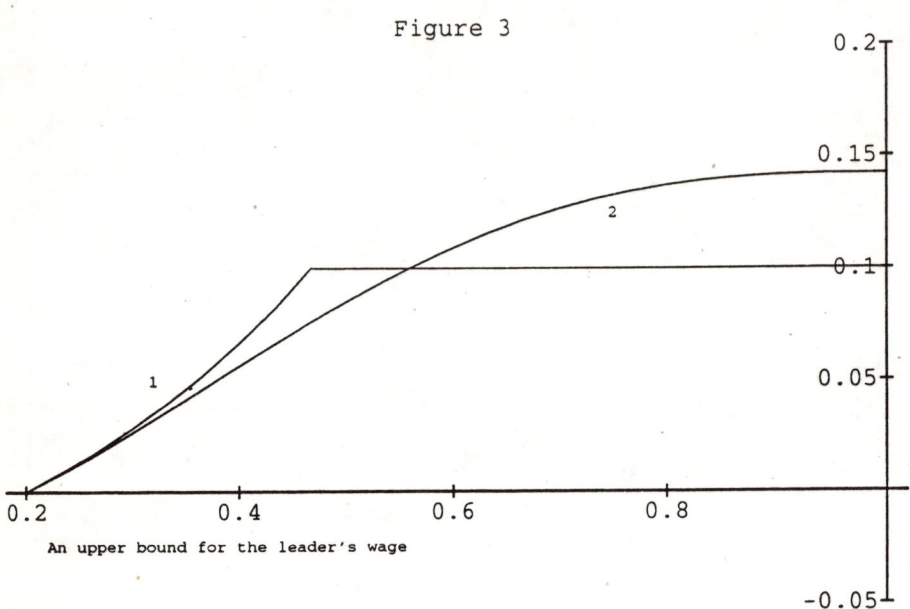

Figure 3

An upper bound for the leader's wage

In the Appendix we show that in this situation beside inequality (2) we also need the following inequality to attain conditions sufficient for preferring independence:

$$w_0 > p - \sum_{j=\frac{n+1}{2}}^{n} \binom{n}{j} p^j (1-p)^{n-j}. \qquad (3)$$

Let us note that if $p \to 1/2$, then the above summation $\to 1/2$, and consequently the right hand side $\to 0$. Thus even though the inequality (3) may not be true for a given p, if p increases it eventually will be true. This reinforces the idea that when p increases, independence becomes more and more convenient.

3. Conclusions

The above analysis has shown that the trade-off between cooperation and independence is not a trivial one. The choice of cooperation versus independence depends, given n (number of members of the decision structure), on several variables, namely: k (the consensus level), p (the probability of accepting a good project), π (the portfolio proportion of good projects), z (the benefit flow originating from a good project), and w the additional salary cost to employ the leader).

If $w = 0$ (no additional cost for the leader) the preferability of a decision structure over another depends only on the respective probabilities $\mathcal{P}^T$ and $\mathcal{P}^I$ of accepting a good project. For the sake of simplicity let us assume n odd and call $(n+1)/2$ the *simple majority rule* (*s.m.r.*). Now

i) if $k < s.m.r.$ then the minimum value of p (p_m) such that $\mathcal{P}^T < \mathcal{P}^I$ is less than $1/2$: $p_m \to 0$ as $k \to 1$;

ii) if $k = s.m.r.$ then $p_m = 1/2$;

iii) if $k > s.m.r.$ then $p_m > 1/2$ and $p_m \to 1$ as $k \to n$ (unanimity).

If $w > 0$ the preferability of one decision structure over the other also depends on π and z. With the *s.m.r.* a necessary condition for preferring cooperation over independence is that $p < 1/2$. As w increases, the interval of the values of p such that cooperation is preferred to independence becomes narrower.

The effect of w on the length of such an interval can be offset by relatively high values of π and z.

Appendix

1. Let us assume that our structure has n members. In the case of independent bureaux they will be denoted with $\{A_i\}$, $i = 1, 2, \ldots, n$. In the case of a team it will be $\{A_i\}$, $i = 1, 2, \ldots, n-1$, and L, where L stands for the leader. The probability of accepting a good project is p for everybody. Furthermore

$$\bar{p} = \mathbf{Pr}[A_i|L] > p,$$

where A_i means the event "A_i accepts a good project", with an analogous meaning for L. The decision of the structure (either team or bureaux) can be reached through different rules. We can speak of different rules of consensus k:

$k = 1$ means that the structure accepts a project if at least one of its members accepts it;

$k = 2$ means that the structure accepts a project if at least two of its members accept; and so on.

$k = n$ means unanimity.

Let $\mathcal{P}^T_{n,k}$ denote the probability that a team with n members and a consensus level k accepts a good project and $\mathcal{P}^I_{n,k}$ the probability that a structure with n independent bureaux with consensus level, k accepts it. Thus

$$\mathcal{P}^I_{n,1} = 1 - (1-p)^n, \qquad \mathcal{P}^I_{n,n} = p^n.$$

To evaluate the analogous probabilities in the case of a team, consider the following relationship:

$$\mathbf{Pr}[A_i | L^c] = \frac{\mathbf{Pr}[A_i \cap L^c]}{\mathbf{Pr}[L^c]} = \frac{(1-\bar{p})p}{1-p} = r \text{ (say)},$$

where the exponent c means complementation.
Then

$$\mathcal{P}^T_{n,1} = 1 - \mathbf{Pr}[A^c_1 \cap A^c_2 \cap \ldots \cap A^c_{n_1} \cap L^c].$$

Henceforth we assume conditional independence; then we get

$$\mathbf{Pr}[A^c_1 \cap A^c_2 \cap \ldots \cap A^c_{n_1} \cap L^c] = \mathbf{Pr}[A^c_1 \cap A^c_2 \cap \ldots \cap A^c_{n_1} | L^c]\mathbf{Pr}[L^c]$$
$$= \mathbf{Pr}[A^c_1|L^c]\mathbf{Pr}[A^c_2|L^c] \times \cdots \times \mathbf{Pr}[A^c_{n-1}|L^c]\mathbf{Pr}[L^c]$$
$$= (1-r)^{n-1}(1-p),$$

and so

$$\mathcal{P}^T_{n,1} = 1 - (1-r)^{n-1}(1-p).$$

Now

$$\bar{p} > p \Rightarrow 1 - \bar{p} < 1 - p \Rightarrow r < p \Rightarrow 1 - r > 1 - p,$$

and so

$$\mathcal{P}^T_{n,1} < \mathcal{P}^I_{n,1}.$$

Analogously

$$\mathcal{P}^T_{n,n} = \mathbf{Pr}[A_1 \cap A_2 \cap \ldots \cap A_{n-1} \cap L]$$
$$= \mathbf{Pr}[A_1 \cap A_2 \cap \ldots \cap A_{n_1}|L]\mathbf{Pr}[L]$$
$$= \bar{p}^{n-1}p,$$

and consequently

$$\mathcal{P}^T_{n,n} > \mathcal{P}^I_{n,n}.$$

For generic n and k, using the laws of probability we get

$$\mathcal{P}^T_{n,k} = \sum_{j=k}^{n-1} \binom{n-1}{j} r^j (1-r)^{n-j-1}(1-p) +$$
$$+ \sum_{j=k}^{n-1} \binom{n-1}{n-j} \bar{p}^{j-1}(1-\bar{p})^{n-j} p + \bar{p}^{n-1} p.$$

Using the binomial relation

$$\binom{n}{m} = \binom{n}{n-m},$$

and making a change of variable the former relation becomes

$$\mathcal{P}^T_{n,k} = \sum_{j=k}^{n-1} \binom{n-1}{j} r^j (1-r)^{n-j-1}(1-p)$$
$$+ \sum_{j=k-1}^{n-1} \binom{n-1}{j} \bar{p}^j (1-\bar{p})^{n-j-1} p.$$

On the other hand

$$\mathcal{P}^I_{n,k} = \sum_{j=k}^{n} \binom{n}{j} p^j (1-p)^{n-j}.$$

For $\bar{p} = p$, $\mathcal{P}^T_{n,k} = \mathcal{P}^I_{n,k}$, as it must be. In fact, when $\bar{p} = p$, then $r = p$ and

$$\mathcal{P}^T_{n,k} = \sum_{j=k}^{n-1} \binom{n-1}{j} p^j (1-p)^{n-j}$$

$$+ \sum_{j=k-1}^{n-1} \binom{n-1}{j} p^{j+1} (1-p)^{n-j-1}$$

$$= \sum_{j=k}^{n-1} \binom{n-1}{j} p^j (1-p)^{n-j} + \sum_{j=k}^{n} \binom{n-1}{j-1} p^j (1-p)^{n-j}$$

$$= \sum_{j=k}^{n-1} \binom{n-1}{j} p^j (1-p)^{n-j}$$

$$+ \sum_{j=k}^{n-1} \binom{n-1}{j-1} p^j (1-p)^{n-j} + p^n$$

$$= \sum_{j=k}^{n-1} \binom{n}{j} p^j (1-p)^{n-j} + p^n$$

$$= \sum_{j=k}^{n} \binom{n}{j} p^j (1-p)^{n-j}$$

$$= \mathcal{P}^I_{n,k}.$$

Another property of $\mathcal{P}^T_{n,k}$ is the following:

$$\bar{p} = 1 \Rightarrow r = 0 \Rightarrow \mathcal{P}^T_{n,k} = p.$$

To get other clear-cut results we confine ourselves to the case where n is odd and $k = (n+1)/2$, that is the simple majority rule.

First of all, if $p = 1/2$ then $r = 1 - \bar{p}$ and

$$\mathcal{P}^T_{n,k} = \frac{1}{2} \sum_{j=\frac{n+1}{2}}^{n-1} \binom{n-1}{j} (1-\bar{p})^j \bar{p}^{n-j-1}$$

$$+ \frac{1}{2} \sum_{j=\frac{n-1}{2}}^{n-1} \binom{n-1}{j} \bar{p}^j (1-\bar{p})^{n-j-1}.$$

But the summation is the probability of at least $(n+1)/2$ successes in $n-1$ Bernoulli trials with success probability equal to $1-\bar{p}$, and so it is equal to the probability of at most $n-1-(n+1)/2 = (n-3)/2$ failures in $n-1$ Bernoulli trials with failure probability equal to $\bar{p}$ and so it proves to be

$$\sum_{j=0}^{\frac{n-3}{2}} \binom{n-1}{j}(1-\bar{p})^j \bar{p}^{n-j-1}.$$

Consequently $\mathcal{P}_{n,k}^T = 1/2$. Obviously $\mathcal{P}_{n,k}^I = 1/2$ and so, for $p = 1/2$, we have $\mathcal{P}_{n,k}^T = \mathcal{P}_{n,k}^I = 1/2$.

To study the behavior of $\mathcal{P}_{n,k}^T$ for other values of p we fix p and consider $\mathcal{P}_{n,k}^T$ as a function of $\bar{p}$. For example, let $p = p_0$. Since $\bar{p} > p$, we are interested in the behavior of $\mathcal{P}_{n,k}^T$ only for values of $\bar{p}$ greater than p_0. We know that for $\bar{p} > p_0$, $\mathcal{P}_{n,k}^T = \mathcal{P}_{n,k}^I$ and clearly $\mathcal{P}_{n,k}^I$ is constant as a function of $\bar{p}$.

So if we can conclude that the first derivative of $\mathcal{P}_{n,k}^T$ with respect to $\bar{p}$ always has the same sign, then for $p = p_0$ the value of $\bar{p}$ for one of the two probabilities is definitively greater than the other one. For example if this derivative is greater than zero then $\mathcal{P}_{n,k}^T > \mathcal{P}_{n,k}^I$.

The first derivative of $\mathcal{P}_{n,k}^T$ with respect to $\bar{p}$ is given by

$$\begin{aligned}\frac{\partial \mathcal{P}_{n,k}^T}{\partial \bar{p}} &= \sum_{j=k}^{n-1} \binom{n-1}{j} [jr^{j-1}(1-r)^{n-j-1} \\ &\quad - (n-j-1)r^j(1-r)^{n-j-2}](-p) \\ &\quad + \sum_{j=k-1}^{n-1} \binom{n-1}{j} [j\bar{p}^{j-1}(1-\bar{p})^{n-j-1} \\ &\quad - (n-j-1)\bar{p}^j(1-\bar{p})^{n-j-2}]p \\ &= pk\binom{n-1}{k}\left[\bar{p}^{k-2}(1-\bar{p})^{k-1} - r^{k-1}(1-r)^{k-2}\right].\end{aligned}$$

This is due to the fact that in the two summations all the terms but the first two cancel out. To see this, consider that, for example,

the first summation can be written as
$$(a_k - b_k) + (a_{k+1} - b_{k+1}) + \ldots + a_{n-1},$$
and
$$b_k = a_{k+1}, \qquad b_{k+1} = a_{k+2},$$
and so on. For example
$$b_k = \binom{n-1}{\frac{n+1}{2}} \frac{n-3}{2} r^{\frac{n+1}{2}} (1-r)^{\frac{n-5}{2}},$$
$$a_{k+1} = \binom{n-1}{\frac{n+3}{2}} \frac{n+3}{2} r^{\frac{n+1}{2}} (1-r)^{\frac{n-5}{2}},$$
and
$$\binom{n-1}{\frac{n+1}{2}} \frac{n-3}{2} = \frac{(n-1)!}{\left(\frac{n+1}{2}\right)! \left(\frac{n-5}{2}\right)!}$$
$$= \binom{n-1}{\frac{n+3}{2}} \frac{n+3}{2}.$$

Setting $r = \gamma(1-\overline{p})$, that is
$$\gamma = \frac{p}{1-p},$$
we get
$$\frac{\partial \mathcal{P}_{n,k}^T}{\partial \overline{p}}$$
$$= pk \binom{n-1}{k} \left[\overline{p}^{k-2}(1-\overline{p}) + \gamma^{k-1}(1-\overline{p})^{k-1}[1-\gamma(1-\overline{p})]^{k-2} \right]$$
$$= pk \binom{n-1}{k} (1-\overline{p})^{k-1} \left[\overline{p}^{k-2} - \gamma^{k-1}[1-\gamma(1-\overline{p})]^{k-2} \right].$$

Now remember that
$$1 - \gamma(1-\overline{p}) = 1 - r > 0.$$

We can write
$$\gamma^{k-1}[1-\gamma(1-\overline{p})]^{k-2} = \left[\gamma^{\frac{k-1}{k-2}} - \gamma^{\frac{2k-3}{k-2}}(1-\overline{p}) \right]^{k-2}.$$

Then

$$\bar{p}^{k-2} - \gamma^{k-1}[1-\gamma(1-\bar{p})]^{k-2} = \left\{\bar{p} - \left[\gamma^{\frac{k-1}{k-2}} - \gamma^{\frac{2k-3}{k-2}}(1-\bar{p})\right]\right\} \times$$
$$\times \text{ (a polynomial of order } k-3\text{)}.$$

This last polynomial turns out to be greater than zero. Consequently the sign of $\frac{\partial \mathcal{P}^T_{n,k}}{\partial \bar{p}}$ depends on the sign of

$$\bar{p} - \gamma^{\frac{k-1}{k-2}} - \gamma^{\frac{2k-3}{k-2}}(1-\bar{p}) = \bar{p}\left[1-\gamma^{\frac{2k-3}{k-2}}\right] + \gamma^{\frac{2k-3}{k-2}} - \gamma^{\frac{k-1}{k-2}}.$$

If $\bar{p} = 0$ then $p = 0$ and consequently $\gamma = 0$. The above quantity is then equal to zero. If $\bar{p} = 1$ then the above quantity is equal to $1 - \gamma^{\frac{k-1}{k-2}}$: if $p < 1/2$ the $\gamma < 1$ and the above quantity is positive; if $p > 1/2$ then $\gamma > 1$ and the above quantity is negative.

Let us assume now $p < 1/2$. Then the above quantity is a straight line with a positive angular coefficient, starting at zero and ending at a value greater than zero in the relevant interval, thus it is always positive.

If $p > 1/2$ then the reverse result is obtained in essentially the same way. To sum up:

if $p < 1/2$ then $\mathcal{P}^T_{n,k} > \mathcal{P}^I_{n,k}$; if $p > 1/2$ then $\mathcal{P}^T_{n,k} < \mathcal{P}^I_{n,k}$.

2. In view of further developments we now specialize to the case $n = 5$ and, as before, $k = (n+1)/2 = 3$. Then

$$\frac{\partial \mathcal{P}^T_{5,3}}{\partial \bar{p}} = 12p\left[\bar{p}(1-\bar{p})^2 - r^2(1-r)\right],$$

$$\frac{\partial^2 \mathcal{P}^T_{5,3}}{\partial \bar{p}^2} = 12p\left\{-2(1-\bar{p})\bar{p} + (1-\bar{p})^2 + \gamma\left[2r(1-r) - r^2\right]\right\}$$
$$= 12p(1-\bar{p})\left[1 - 3\bar{p} + 2\gamma^2 - 3\gamma^3(1-\bar{p})\right].$$

When $\bar{p} = 0$ then $p = 0$ and the second derivative is equal to zero. The same is true when $\bar{p} = 1$. Now consider $0 < \bar{p} < 1$. Set

$$g = g(\bar{p}) = 1 - 3\bar{p} + 2\gamma^2 - 3\gamma^3(1-\bar{p}).$$

Then
$$g(0) = 1 + 2\gamma^2 - 3\gamma^3 = (1-\gamma)(1+\gamma+3\gamma^2),$$
$$g(1) = -2 + 2\gamma^2 = -2(1-\gamma^2).$$

Let $p < 1/2$. Then $0 \leq \gamma < 1$, and $g(0) > 0$, $g(1) < 0$. Furthermore

$$\frac{\partial g}{\partial \bar{p}} = -3 + 3\gamma^3 = -3(1-\gamma^3) < 0.$$

Let $\bar{p}_0$ be the point where $g(\bar{p}_0) = 0$. Then

$$\bar{p}_0 = \frac{1+\gamma+3\gamma^2}{3(1+\gamma+\gamma^2)}.$$

Since
$$1 + \gamma + 3\gamma^2 \geq 1 + \gamma + \gamma^2,$$
it follows that
$$\bar{p}_0 \geq \frac{1}{3}.$$

Since $\bar{p}_0$ is an increasing function of γ, the maximum of $\bar{p}_0$ is reached when $\gamma = 1$ and it is thus equal to 5/9. So

$$\frac{1}{3} \leq \bar{p}_0 \leq \frac{5}{9}.$$

For values of $\bar{p} < \bar{p}_0$, then it turns out $\frac{\partial^2 P^T_{5,3}}{\partial \bar{p}^2} > 0$.

On the other hand, for values of $\bar{p} > \bar{p}_0$, then $\frac{\partial^2 P^T_{5,3}}{\partial \bar{p}^2} < 0$.

3. We formalize the relationship between $\bar{p}$ and p as follows:

$$\bar{p} = \frac{m}{m+1} + \frac{p}{m+1}.$$

Define the salary w as equal to m, let $p = p_0$ and then express m as a function of $\bar{p}$. We get

$$m = \frac{\bar{p} - p_0}{1 - \bar{p}}.$$

Clearly, if $\bar{p} = p_0$ then $m = 0$. If $\bar{p} \to 1$, then $m \to \infty$. The first and second derivative of m with respect to $\bar{p}$ are both positive. Let

$$\Delta(5,3) = 2\pi z(\mathcal{P}_{5,3}^T - \mathcal{P}_{5,3}^I) - w.$$

A necessary condition for $\Delta(5,3) > 0$ is that $\mathcal{P}_{5,3}^T - \mathcal{P}_{5,3}^I > 0$. This happens if $p < 1/2$. So from now on $p_0 < 1/2$. Consider $\Delta(5,3)$ as a function of $\bar{p} \geq p_0$. if $\bar{p} = p_0$, then

$$w = m = 0, \qquad \mathcal{P}_{5,3}^T - \mathcal{P}_{5,3}^I = 0.$$

Numerical calculations show that $\frac{\partial \mathcal{P}_{5,3}^T}{\partial \bar{p}}$ is almost constant up to the point $\bar{p}_0$ of the previous paragraph where the function changes concavity. If $p_0 > \bar{p}_0$, then in the relevant interval the second derivative of $\mathcal{P}_{5,3}^T$ is always negative and the following reasoning is simplified.

In the least favorable situation the quasi-constancy of $\frac{\partial \mathcal{P}_{5,3}^T}{\partial \bar{p}}$ and the behavior of w suggest that a sufficient condition for preferring independence is that the first derivative of $\frac{w}{2\pi z}$ be greater than that of $\mathcal{P}_{5,3}^T - \mathcal{P}_{5,3}^I$ in the same point. We have

$$\frac{\partial \frac{w}{2\pi z}}{\partial \bar{p}} = \frac{(1-p_0)}{2\pi z(1-\bar{p})^2},$$

so that in p_0 is equal to

$$\frac{1}{2\pi z(1-p_0)}.$$

On the other hand

$$\frac{\partial (\mathcal{P}_{5,3}^T - \mathcal{P}_{5,3}^I)}{\partial \bar{p}} = 12p_0 \left[\bar{p}(1-\bar{p})^2 - r_0^2(1-r_0)\right],$$

where $r_0 = \gamma_0(1-\bar{p})$, $\gamma_0 = \frac{p_0}{1-p_0}$.

Consequently this derivative evaluated in $\bar{p} = p_0$ gives

$$12p_0 \left[p_0(1-p_0)^2 - p_0^2(1-p_0)\right].$$

So if
$$\frac{1}{z} > 24\pi p_0^2(1-p_0)^2(1-2p_0)$$
then independence is definitely better.
Since $p_0 < 1/2$, if
$$\frac{1}{z} > 6\pi(1-p_0)^2(1-2p_0)$$
then *a fortiori* independence is preferable. It is clear that as p_0 increases independence becomes ever more preferable.

Now suppose that we have un upper limit to w, say w_0. Recall that if $p = p_0$ then $\mathcal{P}_{5,3}^T$ evaluated in $\bar{p} = 1$ is equal to p_0. Consequently if
$$w_0 > p_0 - \sum_{j=\frac{n+1}{2}}^{n} \binom{n}{j} p_0^j (1-p_0)^{n-j}$$
and
$$z < \frac{1}{6\pi(1-p_0)^2(1-2p_0)},$$
then independence is certainly better.

Let us note that as $p_0 \to 1/2$ the summation in the first inequality tends to $1/2$, and so the right hand side of the first inequality tends to zero. This reinforces the idea that the preferability of independence increases with the value of p_0.

CHAPTER IV

LEADERSHIP AND DEPENDENCE

1. Introduction

The problem we are going to deal with is that of the decision that has to be made by a group of persons (*e.g.* the members of a board or of a committee, the jury in criminal trials). Typically the decision is of a dichotomous type such as whether to accept or reject a project or to absolve or convict a defendant. There is a good deal of literature on the different facets of this problem. Here, more than usual, it is very important to clarify the assumptions made in our analysis. A strong hypothesis is that of the independence of the members, which means that members do not influence one another. A second hypothesis concerns the problem of modelling individual skills. We follow the approach according to which skills may be represented by two numbers, the probabilities of Type I error and of Type II error, or, simply by one number which expresses the probability to make the correct decision.

Many of the principal lines of analysis of this paper have been introduced in the literature. Sah and Stiglitz (*e.g.* 1986, 1988*a*, 1988*b*) presented an analysis of structure (polyarchy, hierarchy or committee) with independence and homogeneity. The same authors discuss the problem of the level of consensus in committees. Nitzan and Paroush (1982) define the optimal weighted majority rule, that is a simple majority rule which associates different weights to the members. In the same context, Karotkin (1993) discusses the inferiority of restricted majority rules (chairman rule, expert rule, etc.). With dependence and homogeneity Berg (1993*a*, 1993*b*, 1994) demonstrates an extension of Condorcet's jury theorem. A simpler model of dependence is given by Boland (1989) and Boland et al. (1989) (deference voting).

In this chapter we construct another, more complex, model of dependence which allows for a certain amount of dishomogeneity. The probabilistic tool used for modelling is that of conditional independence. In this respect our approach is close to that of Berg (who uses the Polya- Eggenberger's urn model). However we also consider the role of the leader who influences the other members. We study the resulting correlation among the members, and how it can be encompassed by a function of the parameters of the model. Then we analyze the distribution of the number of votes of the same type and show that, in the range of values relevant for our parameters, this distribution is bimodal. Finally, we consider a simple scheme of different weighted majority rules and confront them.

2. The model

We are going to make some non-restrictive simplifications. The setup of our model is suggested by an example in Rényi (1970; p. 316). Let us assume that the *project* under scrutiny is good, such that the right decision is to accept it. Our *committee* is composed of one leader and n members. We are going to assume that the n members are among them independent and identical, *conditionally* on the decision made by the leader. Formally, let Ω_1 be the event that the leader accepts the project, and Ω_2 be the event that he refuses it. Thus the two events are disjoint and

$$\Omega_1 \cup \Omega_2 = \Omega, \tag{1}$$

where Ω is the sample space. Furthermore, let A_i denote the event that the i-th member accepts the project, $i = 1, \ldots, n$. Let q_1 be the probability that the leader makes the correct decision; then

$$\mathbf{Pr}[\Omega_i] = q_i \qquad i = 1, 2. \tag{2}$$

Our hypothesis of conditional homogeneity of the members implies that
$$\mathbf{Pr}[A_j|\Omega_i] = p_i \qquad i = 1, 2; \; j = 1, \ldots, n. \tag{3}$$

The hypothesis of conditional independence implies that

$$\mathbf{Pr}[A_{n_1} \cap \ldots \cap A_{n_k}|\Omega_i] = \prod_{i=1}^{k} \mathbf{Pr}[A_{n_i}|\Omega_i] \tag{4}$$
$$= p_i^k,$$

where $n_1 < \ldots < n_k$, $1 \leq k \leq n$. It follows that

$$\mathbf{Pr}[A_{n_1} \cap \ldots \cap A_{n_k}] = \sum_{i=1}^{2} p_i^k q_i = w_k. \tag{5}$$

This result allows us to conclude that the events $\{A_i\}$ are *exchangeable* (see, for example, Rényi (1970; p. 315)). The events $\{A_i\}$ are among them dependent; in fact

$$\mathbf{Pr}[A_j] = \sum_{i=1}^{2} p_i q_i, \quad \text{while} \quad \mathbf{Pr}[A_j|A_i] = \frac{\sum_{i=1}^{2} p_i^2 q_i}{\sum_{i=1}^{2} p_i q_i}. \tag{6}$$

Let us note that $p_1 = p_2$ implies

$$\mathbf{Pr}[A_j|\Omega_1] = \mathbf{Pr}[A_j|\Omega_1^c],$$

where Ω_1^c denotes the complement of Ω_1 and is therefore equal to Ω_2. The latter equality implies the independence of A_j and Ω_i, therefore, if we want the Leader to have an effective influence, we must assume $p_1 \neq p_2$. Furthermore, it is reasonable to assume $p_2 \leq p_1$. It follows that in the sequel we always have $p_2 < p_1$. We are going to assume that $p_1 > 1/2$, $p_2 < 1/2$.

Now let α_i be the indicator of the event A_i. Consequently all the random variables $\{\alpha_i\}$ have the same marginal distribution. It is easy to obtain the expected value and the variance

$$\mathbf{E}[\alpha_i] = \sum_{i=1}^{2} p_i q_i, \quad \mathbf{V}[\alpha_i] = \sum_{i=1}^{2} p_i q_i - \left(\sum_{i=1}^{2} p_i q_i\right)^2. \quad (7)$$

3. Correlation among the members

The coefficient of linear correlation ρ between α_i and α_j is given by

$$\rho = \frac{\sum_{i=1}^{2} p_i^2 q_i - \left(\sum_{i=1}^{2} p_i q_i\right)^2}{\sum_{i=1}^{2} p_i q_i - \left(\sum_{i=1}^{2} p_1 q_i\right)^2}. \quad (8)$$

Let us note that $\rho \geq 0$, since the numerator in (8) is the variance of the numbers $\{p_i\}$. Furthermore $\rho = 0$ when $p_1 = p_2$, which is obvious given what was said previously. The numerator in (8) is just the covariance between α_i and α_j. The same previous considerations show that this covariance is an increasing function of $|p_1 - p_2|$ or, in our model, simply of $p_1 - p_2$. This allows us to consider the difference $p_1 - p_2$ as *a measure of the dependence among the members*.

As far as ρ is concerned we can prove the following proposition.

Proposition 1. Let us assume that $p_1 > 1/2$, $p_2 < 1/2$, $q = q_1 \geq 1/2$ and furthermore $p_1 + p_2 \geq 1$. Then ρ is an increasing function of $p_1 - p_2$.

Proof. To simplify matters, let $1 - q = q_2$ and write

$$A = \sum_{i=1}^{2} p_i q_i,$$

$$B = \sum_{i=1}^{2} p_i^2 q_i.$$

Then
$$\rho = \frac{B - A^2}{A - A^2},$$
and
$$A^2 \leq B \leq A.$$

The numerator of $\frac{\partial \rho}{\partial p_1}$ can be written, after dividing by q, as
$$D = 2p_1 A - 2p_1 A^2 - A^2 - B + 2AB.$$

If we set $p_1 = 1/2$ we get
$$D > A - 2A^2 - B + 2AB$$
$$= (A - B)(1 - 2A).$$

Now, with $p_1 = 1/2$ we have
$$1 - 2A = 1 - q + 2qp_2 - 2p_2$$
$$= (1 - q)(1 - 2p_2) \quad > \quad 0.$$

So we conclude that ρ is an increasing function of p_1. Working along the same lines we can also conclude that ρ is a decreasing function of p_2. Now let $p_1 - p_2 = \varepsilon$. It is clear, using the previous results, that if p_1 increases and p_2 decreases then ε decreases as does ρ. The opposite happens when p_1 decreases and p_2 increases. Now we analyse what happens when p_1 and p_2 both increase (or both decrease). To begin with, let us assume that both increase of the quantity h, $0 \leq h \leq 1 - p_1$, so that ε does not change. That is to say we put
$$p_1^\star = p_1 + h, \qquad p_2^\star = p_2 + h,$$
and denote with $\rho^\star$ the corresponding ρ. Then the numerator of $\rho^\star$ is unchanged with respect to that of ρ (since the variance is unaffected by translations), while the denominator is now
$$A - A^2 + h - h^2 - 2hA.$$

So $\rho^\star > \rho$ if
$$h - h^2 - 2hA < 0,$$

or
$$1 - 2A < h.$$
First of all, let us note that
$$1 - 2A < 1 - p_1,$$
so that the above inequality makes sense with the restriction imposed on h. We have
$$2A - p_1 = 2q(p_1 - p_2) + 2p_2 - p_1$$
$$\geq p_2 > 0,$$
since $q \geq 1/2$. Now if $1 - 2A \leq 0$ we can conclude that for every positive $h < 1 - p_1$ always $\rho^* > \rho$. We have that
$$1 - 2A = 1 - 2qp_1 + 2qp_2 - 2p_2 < 0,$$
if
$$q > \frac{1}{2} \frac{1 - 2p_2}{p_1 - p_2}.$$
A sufficient condition for the above inequality to be true is
$$p_1 + p_2 \geq 1,$$
which was assumed to hold.

Now let
$$\bar{p}_1 = p_1 + h, \quad \bar{p}_2 = p_2 + k, \quad k < h,$$
so that
$$\bar{p}_1 - \bar{p}_2 = \varepsilon + h - k = \bar{\varepsilon}.$$
Then
$$\bar{p}_1 = p_1^*, \quad \bar{p}_2 < p_2^*, \quad \bar{\varepsilon} > \varepsilon,$$
and we can conclude that
$$\bar{\rho} > \rho^* > \rho.$$
This proves that ρ is an increasing function of $p_1 - p_2$ under the assumptions of the proposition.

4. Distribution of the number of votes

Now let β be the indicator of the event Ω_1 and let us define the variable S_n as follows

$$S_n = \beta + \alpha_1 + \ldots + \alpha_n, \tag{9}$$

that is, S_n is the number of members (including the Leader) who vote to accept the project. We have

$$\mathbf{E}[S_n] = q_1 + n \sum_{i=1}^{2} p_i q_i, \tag{10}$$

$$\mathbf{V}[S_n] = q_1 q_2 + n \mathbf{V}[\alpha_i] + 2 \sum_{i=1}^{n} \mathbf{Cov}[\beta, \alpha_i] + \sum_{i=1}^{n} \sum_{j \neq i} \mathbf{Cov}[\alpha_i, \alpha_j], \tag{11}$$

where

$$\mathbf{Cov}[\beta, \alpha_i] = p_1 q_1 - q_1 \mathbf{E}[\alpha_i].$$

Since $q_1 + q_2 = 1$, writing q for q_1 we get

$$\mathbf{Pr}[S_n = 0] = (1-q)(1-p_2)^n,$$

$$\mathbf{Pr}[S_n = k] = q \binom{n}{k-1} p_1^{k-1}(1-p_1)^{n-k+1} \tag{12}$$
$$+ (1-q) \binom{n}{k} p_2^k (1-p_2)^{n-k} \qquad 1 \leq k \leq n,$$

$$\mathbf{Pr}[S_n = n+1] = q p_1^n.$$

The following *Proposition 2* sheds some light on the form of the distribution of S_n.

Proposition 2. Let q and n be given. Then there exists a range of values of p_1 and of p_2 such that the distribution of S_n exhibits a relative minimum for $k = \frac{n}{2}$. This means that the distribution is (at least) bimodal.

Proof. As we said, it is reasonable to assume $p_1 > \frac{1}{2}$, $p_2 < \frac{1}{2}$. This implies

$$\frac{n}{2} < p_1(n+1). \qquad (\star)$$

Furthermore let us assume, for the sake of simplicity, that n is even. Let us write

$$\mathcal{P}_k = \mathbf{Pr}[S_n = k]$$
$$= q\binom{n}{k-1}p_1^{k-1}(1-p_1)^{n-k+1} + (1-q)\binom{n}{k}p_2^k(1-p_2)^{n-k},$$

for $1 \leq k \leq n$. Then

$$\mathcal{P}_{\frac{n}{2}-1} = q\binom{n}{\frac{n}{2}-2}p_1^{\frac{n}{2}-2}(1-p_1)^{\frac{n}{2}+2}$$
$$+ (1-q)\binom{n}{\frac{n}{2}-1}p_2^{\frac{n}{2}-1}(1-p_2)^{\frac{n}{2}+1},$$

$$\mathcal{P}_{\frac{n}{2}} = q\binom{n}{\frac{n}{2}-1}p_1^{\frac{n}{2}-1}(1-p_1)^{\frac{n}{2}+1} + (1-q)\binom{n}{\frac{n}{2}}p_2^{\frac{n}{2}}(1-p_2)^{\frac{n}{2}},$$

$$\mathcal{P}_{\frac{n}{2}+1} = q\binom{n}{\frac{n}{2}}p_1^{\frac{n}{2}}(1-p_1)^{\frac{n}{2}} + (1-q)\binom{n}{\frac{n}{2}+1}p_2^{\frac{n}{2}+1}(1-p_2)^{\frac{n}{2}-1}.$$

To prove this proposition we have to prove that it is possible to find a range of values of p_1 and of p_2 such that

$$\mathcal{P}_{\frac{n}{2}-1} > \mathcal{P}_{\frac{n}{2}},$$
$$\mathcal{P}_{\frac{n}{2}+1} > \mathcal{P}_{\frac{n}{2}}.$$

With a little algebra we get that if the first inequality is true then

$$\frac{q}{1-q}\left(\frac{p_1}{p_2}\right)^{\frac{n}{2}-2}\left(\frac{1-p_1}{1-p_2}\right)^{\frac{n}{2}}\frac{1-p_1}{p_2}\frac{\frac{n}{2}-1-p_1(n+1)}{\frac{n}{2}+2} >$$
$$> \frac{p_2(n+1)-\frac{n}{2}}{\frac{n}{2}}.$$

If this last one holds, then, because of $(\star)$ it has to be

$$p_2(n+1) < \frac{n}{2}.$$

On the other hand, if the second inequality is true then

$$\frac{q}{1-q}\left(\frac{p_1}{p_2}\right)^{\frac{n}{2}-1}\left(\frac{1-p_1}{1-p_2}\right)^{\frac{n}{2}-1}\frac{1-p_1}{p_2}\frac{-\frac{n}{2}+p_1(n+1)}{\frac{n}{2}+1} > $$
$$> \frac{-p_2(n+1)+\frac{n}{2}+1}{\frac{n}{2}+1}.$$

Writing

$$Q = \left(\frac{p_1}{p_2}\right)^{\frac{n}{2}-2}\left(\frac{1-p_1}{1-p_2}\right)^{\frac{n}{2}-1}\frac{q}{1-q}\frac{1-p_1}{p_2},$$

the first inequality becomes

$$Q\frac{1-p_1}{1-p_2}\frac{\frac{n}{2}-1-p_1(n+1)}{\frac{n}{2}+2} > \frac{p_2(n+1)-\frac{n}{2}}{\frac{n}{2}},$$

while the second one becomes

$$Q\frac{p_1}{p_2}\frac{-\frac{n}{2}+p_1(n+1)}{\frac{n}{2}+1} > \frac{-p_2(n+1)+\frac{n}{2}+1}{\frac{n}{2}+1}.$$

Now using $(\star)$ we can write

$$Q < \frac{1-p_2}{1-p_1}\frac{\frac{n}{2}+2}{\frac{n}{2}-1-p_1(n+1)}\frac{p_2(n+1)-\frac{n}{2}}{\frac{n}{2}},$$

$$Q > \frac{p_2}{p_1}\frac{\frac{n}{2}+1}{p_1(n+1)-\frac{n}{2}}\frac{-p_2(n+1)+\frac{n}{2}+1}{\frac{n}{2}+1}.$$

Let us set

$$A = \frac{1-p_2}{1-p_1}\frac{\frac{n}{2}+2}{\frac{n}{2}-1-p_1(n+1)}\frac{p_2(n+1)-\frac{n}{2}}{\frac{n}{2}},$$

$$B = \frac{p_2}{p_1}\frac{\frac{n}{2}+1}{p_1(n+1)-\frac{n}{2}}\frac{-p_2(n+1)+\frac{n}{2}+1}{\frac{n}{2}+1}.$$

In Fig. 1 we set $n = 10$, $q = 0.6$, $p_1 = 0.75$: A, B, Q are drawn as functions of p_2.

B is a continuous function of p_1 and p_2: since for $p_1 = 1$ and $p_2 \geq 0$ we have $B < 1$, that means that there exists a p_1^* such that for $p_1 > p_1^*$ and for all the p_2 of interest one gets $B < 1$. Furthermore

$$\lim_{p_2 \to 0} Q = +\infty,$$

$$\lim_{p_2 \to 0} A = finite,$$

$$\lim_{p_2 \to \frac{n}{2(n+1)}} A = 0.$$

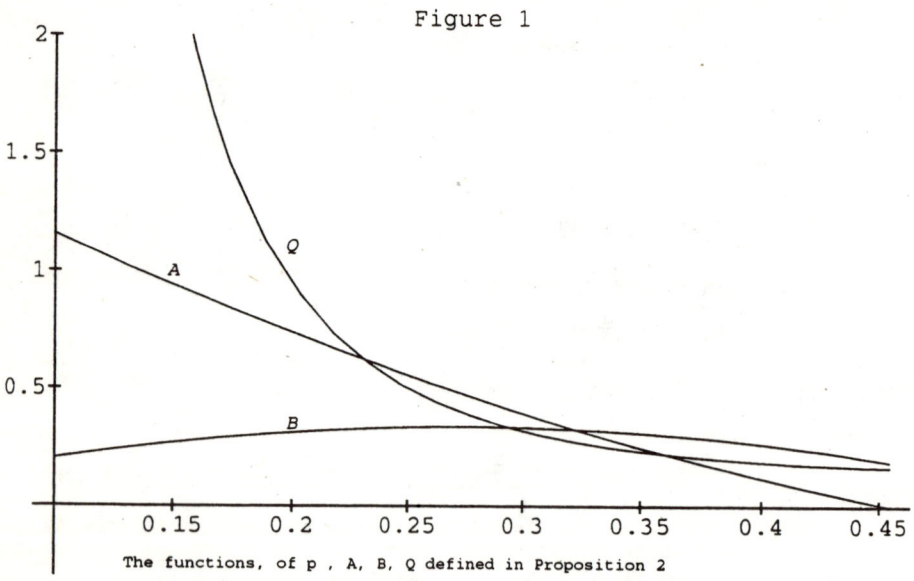

Figure 1

The functions, of p , A, B, Q defined in Proposition 2

Let p_2^* be the solution to the equation $Q = 1$ in p_2 as a function of p_1. We can verify that this solution $\to 0$ as p_1 increases. That means that there exists a $\bar{p}_1$ such that for $p_1 > \bar{p}_1$, for all $p_2 < p_2^*$ one has: $Q > 1$; furthermore $Q = A$ for $p_2 = \bar{p}_2 < p_2^*$. Combining all these results it follows that for

$$\bar{p}_2 < p_2 < p_2^*,$$

$$p_1 > \max(\bar{p}_1, p_1^*),$$

we have
$$A > Q > B,$$
as it was to be proved.

Remark. This proof suggests that as difference $p_1 - p_2$ decreases, the bimodal form tends to disappear. As we have seen, this difference measures the dependence among members. We can therefore conclude that the bimodal form of the distribution of S_n is an increasing function of the dependence among the members. Fig. 2, obtained with $n = 10$, $q = 0.6$, $p_1 = 0.75$, gives the distribution of S_n for different values of p_2, which are written at the top of the corresponding curve.

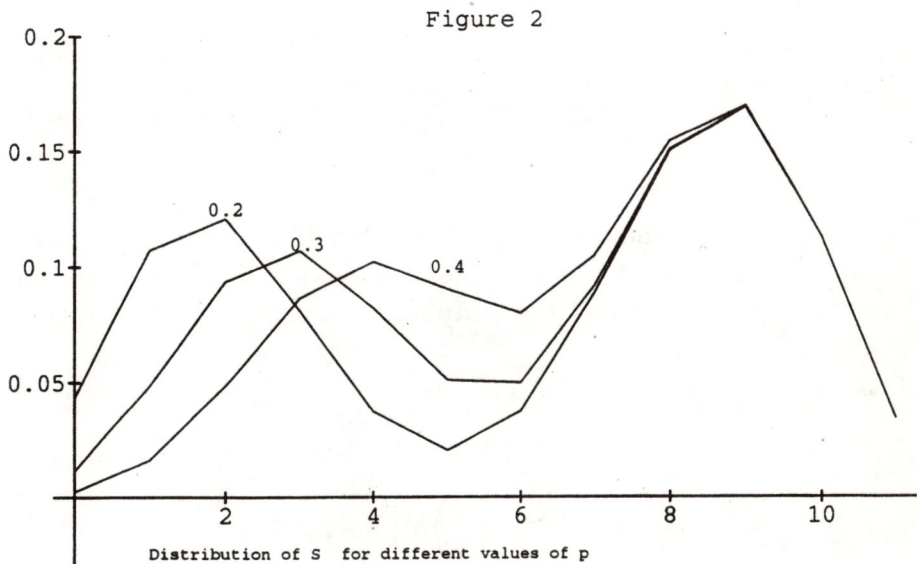

Figure 2

Distribution of S for different values of p

5. Performance under different majority rules

Now we want to study the performance of a committee with the above outlined characteristics. Let us assume that the required majority is the simple majority. We consider two different situations: one not weighted (that is, all the members including the leader have the same weight), and another one where we assign more weight to the leader than to the other members. Let us suppose that each member (including the leader) possesses one vote. To simplify, let n be even and let r, again an even integer, be the augmented number of votes that the leader might possess. It has to be $0 \leq r \leq n$. With $r = 0$ we have a uniform distribution of the weights, with $r = n$ the leader will always be the majority and so the decision of the committee is going to be the leader's decision. Under this framework, let us denote as $B_{n,r}$ the event that a committee composed of n members and one leader, with a distribution of weights r, takes the right decision, according to the rule of simple majority. Then

$$\mathbf{Pr}[B_{n,r}] = q \sum_{i=\frac{n-r}{2}}^{n} \binom{n}{i} p_1^i (1-p_1)^{n-i} \qquad (13)$$

$$+ (1-q) \sum_{i=\frac{n+r}{2}+1}^{n} \binom{n}{i} p_2^i (1-p_2)^{n-i}.$$

We want to study the behavior of this probability in two situations: when n increases and r is kept fixed; and when n is kept constant and r is allowed to vary. For simplicity let us set $P_{n,r} = \mathbf{Pr}[B_{n,r}]$ and

$$s_1 = \sum_{i=\frac{n-r}{2}}^{n} \binom{n}{i} p_1^i (1-p_1)^{n-i},$$

$$s_2 = \sum_{i=\frac{n+r}{2}+1}^{n} \binom{n}{i} p_2^i (1-p_2)^{n-i}.$$

Beginning with the first situation let $r = 0$ and, as always, $p_2 < p_1$.
1. If $p_1 > 1/2$, then s_1 increases with n and
   (a) if $p_2 < 1/2$, s_2 decreases and if $p_1 \leq q$ then $P_{n,0}$ steadily increases and $\to q$ with $n \to \infty$.
   (b) If $p_2 < 1/2$ and $p_1 > q$, $P_{n,0}$ at the beginning increases and then decreases to q as $n \to \infty$. For the initial values of n we might have $P_{n,0} < q$.

(c) If $p_2 = 1/2$ then $P_{n,0}$ steadily increases and its limit for $n \to \infty$ is $\frac{q+1}{2}$. For the initial values of n it may be the case that $P_{n,0} < q$.

(d) If $p_2 > 1/2$, what is said in sub-item (c) holds *a fortiori* and $\lim_{n\to\infty} P_{n,0} = 1$.

2. If $p_1 = 1/2$, $p_2 < 1/2$ then it is always true that $P_{n,0} < q$ and this quantity after the initial values of n increases steadily toward $\frac{q}{2}$ which is its limit for $n \to \infty$.

3. If $p_1 < 1/2$ the above result holds *a fortiori*, naturally with $p_2 < p_1$: $P_{n,0}$ decreases steadily toward 0 with $n \to \infty$.

Items 2 and 3 are a consequence of the following *Proposition*.

Proposition 3. If $p_1 = p_2 = 1/2$ and if $q \geq 1/2$, then $P_{n,0} \leq q$; on the contrary, if $q < 1/2$, then $P_{n,0} > q$.

Proof. With $p_1 = p_2 = 1/2$ we have

$$P_{n,0} = q \sum_{i=\frac{n}{2}}^{n} \frac{1}{2^n} \binom{n}{i} + (1-q) \sum_{i=\frac{n}{2}+1}^{n} \frac{1}{2^n} \binom{n}{i}$$

$$= \frac{q}{2^n} S_1 + \frac{1-q}{2^n} S_2$$

$$= \frac{1}{2^n} [qS_1 + S_2 - qS_2]$$

$$= \frac{1}{2^n} [q(S_1 - S_2) + S_2]$$

$$= \frac{1}{2^n} \left[q \binom{n}{\frac{n}{2}} + S_2 \right].$$

On the other hand, a look at the Tartaglia's (Pascal's) Triangle shows that

$$S_2 = \frac{2^n - \binom{n}{\frac{n}{2}}}{2},$$

whence

$$P_{n,0} = \frac{1}{2^n} \left[\binom{n}{\frac{n}{2}} \left(q - \frac{1}{2} \right) + 2^{n-1} \right]$$

$$= \frac{1}{2^n} \binom{n}{\frac{n}{2}} \left(q - \frac{1}{2} \right) + \frac{1}{2}.$$

This one yields
$$P_{n,0} - q = \left(q - \frac{1}{2}\right)\left[\frac{1}{2^n}\binom{n}{\frac{n}{2}} - 1\right].$$

Considering that
$$\frac{1}{2^n}\binom{n}{\frac{n}{2}} - 1 < 0,$$

we obtain the desired result.

Now we want to study the behavior of $P_{n,r}$ keeping n fixed and varying r. To this end, let us set $r = k$, $k = 0, 2, \ldots, n-2$, and

$$S_1^k = \sum_{i=\frac{n-k}{2}}^{n} \binom{n}{i} p_1^i (1-p_1)^{n-i},$$

$$S_2^k = \sum_{i=\frac{n+k}{2}+1}^{n} \binom{n}{i} p_2^i (1-p_2)^{n-i}.$$

Then
$$P_{n,k} - P_{n,k+2} = qS_1^k + (1-q)S_2^k - qS_1^{k+2} - (1-q)S_2^{k+2}$$
$$= q\left[S_1^k - S_1^{k+2} + S_2^{k+2} - S_2^k\right] + S_2^k - S_2^{k+2}$$
$$= (1-q)\binom{n}{\frac{n+k}{2}+1} p_2^{\frac{n+k}{2}+1}(1-p_2)^{\frac{n-k}{2}-1} +$$
$$\quad - q\binom{n}{\frac{n-k}{2}-1} p_1^{\frac{n-k}{2}-1}(1-p_1)^{\frac{n+k}{2}+1}.$$

So it is clear that the sign of $P_{n,k} - P_{n,k+2}$ depends on the sign of

$$(1-q)p_2^{\frac{n+k}{2}+1}(1-p_2)^{\frac{n-k}{2}-1} - qp_1^{\frac{n-k}{2}-1}(1-p_1)^{\frac{n+k}{2}+1},$$

since the two binomial coefficients that appear above are equal. Let us fix $q > 1/2$ and $p_1 > 1/2$. Now let us consider the equation in p_2

$$p_2^{\frac{n+k}{2}+1}(1-p_2)^{\frac{n-k}{2}-1} = \frac{q}{1-q} p_1^{\frac{n-k}{2}-1}(1-p_1)^{\frac{n+k}{2}+1}. \qquad (14)$$

To simplify the analysis let us suppose $p_2 < 1/2$ e $p_1 > q$, which seems to be reasonable.

Let us note that $f(p) = p^h(1-p)^{n-h}$ is an increasing function of p if $\frac{h}{n} > p$; otherwise on the contrary if $\frac{h}{n} < p$ it is a decreasing function of p. In (14) let us set $p_2 = 1/2$. Then the left hand side is equal to $\frac{1}{2^n}$. The right hand side can be rewritten as

$$\frac{q}{1-q} \frac{1-p_1}{p_1} p_1^{\frac{n-k}{2}} (1-p_1)^{\frac{n+k}{2}},$$

where, given our assumptions, the product of the first two factors is less than one. Let us set $h = \frac{n-k}{2}$. Then

$$\frac{h}{n} < \frac{1}{2} < p_1,$$

and the right hand side is a decreasing function of p_1. If $p_1 = 1/2$ the right hand side is less than $\frac{1}{2^n}$ and so its value is even lower when $p_1 > 1/2$. We can conclude that for $p_2 = 1/2$ the left hand side is greater than the right hand one. Otherwise, when $p_2 = 0$, it is clear that the inequality is reverted. Thus, there exists a solution to the equation (14) with $p_2 < 1/2$. Let us denote this solution with p_2^k. As for the left hand side, the same line of reasoning allows us to conclude that, for $p_2 < 1/2$, it is an increasing function of p_2. Consequently, for $p_2 > p_2^k$, we get

$$P_{n,k} > P_{n,k+2}.$$

Let us now see how p_2^k varies when varying k. Let $f(h) = p^h(1-p)^{n-h}$. Taking the logarithm and then the derivative we see that $f(h)$ is an increasing function of h if $p > 1-p$, and a decreasing function if $p < 1-p$. On the other hand, if $f(h) = p^{n-h}(1-p)^h$, then $f(h)$ is an increasing function of h if $p < 1-p$.

Combining all this and the fact that $p_1 > 1/2$, we can conclude that the right hand side of (14) is a decreasing function of k. Using the fact that $p_2 < 1/2$, we observe that the left hand side is an increasing function of k. So if the equality in (14) must hold with an increase of k, we must choose p_2 in such a way as to sufficiently reduce the left hand side. Since the left hand side is an increasing function of p_2, then, if k increases, the solution to (14) p_2^k decreases.

Consequently
$$p_2^0 \geq p_2^2 \geq \ldots \geq p_2^{n-2}.$$
It follows that for $p_2 \geq p_2^0$
$$P_{n,0} > P_{n,2} > \ldots > P_{n,n-2}.$$
Reverting the reasoning we have that for $p_2 \leq p_2^{n-2}$
$$P_{n,0} < P_{n,2} < \ldots < P_{n,n-2}.$$

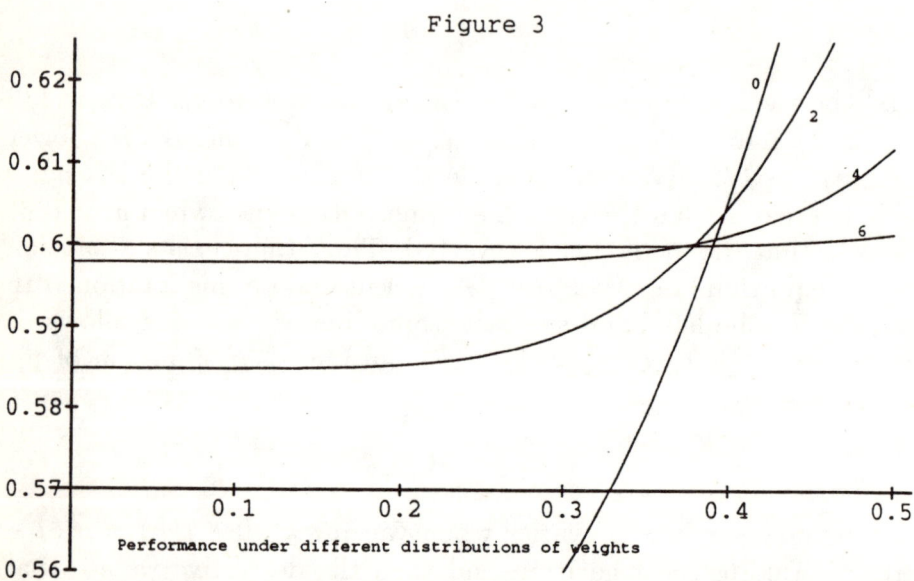

Figure 3

Performance under different distributions of weights

Our conclusion is that outside the interval $[p_2^{n-2}, p_2^0]$ there is no room for ambiguity. More precisely, on the left of this interval the maximum is attained for $r = n$, while on the right it is attained for $r = 0$. Values ranging within this interval do not allow for a clear-cut conclusion. Fig. 3 illustrates this. In Fig. 3 we set $n = 8$, $q = 0.6$, $p_1 = 0.65$. The curves represent $P_{n,r}$ as a function of p_2 for different values of r, which are written close to the corresponding curve.

CHAPTER V

THE DECISION MAKING PROCESS OF POLITICAL ORGANIZATIONS

1. Introduction

In this chapter we are going to analyse the decision making process of political organizations, exploiting the pioneering ideas of Sah and Stiglitz.

In a series of contributions Sah and Stiglitz (1985; 1986; 1988a; 1988b) analyze the problem of how different decision structures such as committees, polyarchies, and hierarchies approach decision making, and how they compare in terms of efficiency. The same authors study the case where a dichotomous choice has to be made. To assess relative performance, Sah and Stiglitz resort to probabilistic tools. They assume that the n members of the structure are independent among themselves and homogeneous with respect to their skills. Furthermore, they represent the skills through the probability of accepting a good project and the probability of rejecting a bad one. The project under scrutiny is drawn from a portfolio of projects whose composition in terms of good and bad projects is known to all the members.

Even if the three mentioned structures are formally different, from a probabilistic point of view polyarchies and hierarchies can both be considered as particular cases of committees. Committees are characterized by a level of *consensus*, let us say h. A committee makes a decision if at least h members agree on it. Imagine the committee acting sequentially. A polyarchy is then a committee whose consensus level is $h = 1$, while a hierarchy is a committee whose consensus level is $h = n$.

Sah and Stiglitz compare the different decision structures in terms of two components of efficiency: the precision, which is measured by the probability of making the right decision, and a cost related to the time required to reach the decision. They formalize this last point considering the expected number of evaluations a project must pass before a decision is taken. This is a variable only for hierarchies and polyarchies, since in the case of a committee all the members assess the project simultaneously.

In this chapter we are going to analyze the above mentioned elements, but most importantly we are going to relax the assumption of independence. To do so, we use the Polya-Eggenberger's urn model. This idea was suggested by papers of Berg (1993a, 1993b, 1994), who studied Condorcet's jury theorem in the presence of dependence among the jurors. Herein, we study the effect of the dependence on the two mentioned components of efficiency.

2. A model of dependence within decision structures

One possible method of visualizing the dependence relationship among the members of a decision structure is to consider the decision process of the restricted political committee of a western party. Each member of the committee belonging to the same party share the same ideology (the ultimate goals), but we can assume that within the committee they act independently from each other.

We can further assume that different parties have different ideological cohesion strength. Consider, for example, a party composed of different, individually homogeneous, factions. Hence, conditionally upon belonging to same party the factions act independently, but unconditionally they are dependent. The amount of dependence is determined by the level of the cohesion strength of the party. The stronger the cohesion, the greater the dependence.

From a probabilistic point of view this situation can be described in terms of dependence coupled with conditional independence. The easiest way to model this phenomenon is to resort to Polya-Eggenberger's urn model. This is the tool we are going to use to study the efficiency (as defined in Section 1) of the decision process of our political committee when it follows the rules either of hierarchy or of polyarchy. More precisely, both for hierarchy and polyarchy, we are going to analyse how and to what extent the type of dependence introduced above affects the probability of making the right decision, as well as the expected number of evaluations in comparison with the known results in the case of independence.

There are two ways to derive the Polya-Eggenberger urn model. Let us consider an urn containing b black balls and w white balls. We draw one ball from the urn and then we replace the ball into the urn along with other k balls of the same color and continue this process, always adding after each drawing, k balls of the same color of that drawn. The number of black balls obtained in n drawings is said to follow the *Polya distribution*. k is a parameter which measures the dependence among the outcomes. In our context, it can interpreted as a measure of the cohesion strength of the party. If $k = 0$ the Polya distribution is simply the binomial distribution. In this case we have independence. If $k = -1$ we get hypergeometric distribution. If $k > 0$ the Polya-Eggenberger urn model, as described above, is equivalent to the stochastic process generated by a sequence of Bernoulli trials, where the probability of success follows a beta distribution. This is the reason why sometimes Polya distribution is sometimes also known as beta-binomial distribution.

3. Polyarchies and hierarchies

In what follows, by the term project we intend any dichotomous choice that the restricted political committee has to make.

3a. Polyarchies

In a polyarchy, a project is selected randomly from a portfolio containing good and bad projects and is then analysed by one member of the structure. If this member accepts the project, the entire structure accepts it; otherwise, the project is returned to the portfolio for possible scrutiny by another member, and so on. Probabilistically, this is equivalent to a sequential process whereby a project undergoes a sequence of examinations by the members of the committee until one member accepts it (if there exists such a member).

Our political committee will be composed of n members. Let us assume that the project to be scrutinised is good (the same arguments can be used if the project is bad, with appropriate changes in notation. In this case the right decision is to accept it. Let p be the individual probability to accept a good project, or in our case the individual probability to make the right decision. Denoting with P_{A_I} the probability that a structure with independence makes the right decision with P_{A_I} and the same probability in the case of our political committee with P_{A_D}, in Appendix 2 it is shown that

$$P_{A_I} > P_{A_D},$$

that is, the probability to make the right decision is always greater in the absence of dependence. The difference $P_{A_I} - P_{A_D}$ increases as ideological cohesion increases.

Now consider the expected number of evaluations a project must undergo. Let us call this number of evaluations N_I and N_D respectively, for the model with independence and for the model with dependence. As shown in Appendix 2,

$$\mathbf{E}[N_D] > \mathbf{E}[N_I],$$

that is, the expected number of evaluations is always greater in the case of dependence. The difference $\mathbf{E}[N_D] - \mathbf{E}[N_I]$ increases as the ideological cohesion increases.

3b. Hierarchies

Let the assumptions be the same as in Section 3a. In a hierarchy a project is accepted only if all the members of the decision structure accept it. Probabilistically, this is equivalent to a sequential process whereby a project undergoes a sequence of evaluations until a first member rejects it (if there exists such a member). Denoting with $P^\star_{A_I}$ and with $P^\star_{A_D}$, the probability to make the right decision for a structure with independence and, respectively, dependence, we show in Appendix 2 that

$$P^\star_{A_D} > P^\star_{A_I},$$

that is, the probability to make the right decision is always greater in the case of dependence. The difference $P^\star_{A_D} - P^\star_{A_I}$ increases as the cohesion increases.

As for the expected number of evaluations we have

$$\mathbf{E}[N^\star_D] > \mathbf{E}[N^\star_I],$$

where $N^\star_D$ is the expected number of evaluations in the case of dependence and $N^\star_I$ is that in the case of independence. So the expected number of evaluations is always greater in the case of dependence. The difference, as always, increases as the cohesion increases.

6. Conclusions

In this chapter we studied the effect of the introduction of dependence among the members of a decision making structure on the probability to make the right decision, and on the expected number of evaluations a project must pass before a decision is taken. The dependence was introduced through the scheme of the Polya-Eggenberger urn model. A parameter of this model can be assumed as a measure of the dependence. The decision making structures considered are, as for Sah and Stiglitz, polyarchies, hierarchies and committees (for simplicity we consider only committees whose consensus level is equal to 2). In the case of polyarchies and hierarchies we got very clear results. In both structures, the expected number of evaluations increases with dependence. In the case of polyarchies, on the other hand, the probability to make the right decision decreases as dependence increases, while the contrary is true for hierarchies. As for committees, the results are less evident. The behavior of the expected number of evaluations, as a function of the parameter measuring dependence, depends on the individual precision or skill, measured by the individual probability to make the right decision. What we can say is that with high individual precision this expected number is an increasing function of dependence, while in the case of low individual precision the opposite is true. Moving from high individual precision to low individual precision we have a combination of the mentioned behaviors.

Appendix 1

Given the definition of the generalized ascending factorials, if $h, k > 0$, $h > k$, we have

$$\frac{p^{[h,\varphi]}}{p^{[k,\varphi]}} = (p + k\varphi)^{[h-k,\varphi]}.$$

Suppose now that $h < k$. Then

$$(p + k\varphi)^{[-(k-h),\varphi]} =$$

$$= \frac{1}{(p + h\varphi)(p + (h+1)\varphi)\cdots(p + (k-1)\varphi)}$$

$$= \frac{p + k\varphi}{(p + k\varphi)(p + k\varphi - \varphi)(p + k\varphi - 2\varphi)\cdots(p + k\varphi - (k-h)\varphi)}$$

$$= \frac{p + k\varphi}{(p + k\varphi)^{[k-h+1,-\varphi]}},$$

and this is definite if

$$\varphi \neq p, \frac{p}{2}, \ldots, \frac{p}{k-h}.$$

So generally, if $r > 0$, $\varphi > 0$ and $\varphi \neq p, \frac{p}{2}, \ldots, \frac{p}{r}$,

$$p^{[-r,\varphi]} = \frac{p}{p^{[r+1,-\varphi]}}.$$

As a consequence
$$p^{[r,-\varphi]} p^{[-r,\varphi]} = \frac{p}{p-r\varphi}.$$

Appendix 2

Let α_i denote the indicator of the event that the i-th drawing turned out to be a black ball. Let us suppose that the number of drawings is n. Then
$$S_n = \sum_{i=1}^{n} \alpha_i$$
is the number of black balls obtained in n drawings. The distribution of S_n is called the *Polya distribution* (see *e.g* Feller (1968; p. 142)); with a reparametrisation it can be written in the following form
$$\mathbf{Pr}[S_n = x] = \binom{n}{x} \frac{p^{[x,\varphi]} q^{[n-x,\varphi]}}{1^{[n,\varphi]}}, \qquad x = 0, 1, \ldots, n$$
where
$$p = \frac{b}{b+w}, \qquad q = 1 - p, \qquad \varphi = \frac{k}{b+w},$$
$$\varphi > \max\left(\frac{-p}{n-1}, \frac{-q}{n-1}\right),$$
and we introduced the generalized ascending factorials, defined for integer x,
$$p^{[x,\varphi]} = p(p+\varphi)(p+2\varphi) \cdots (p+(x-1)\varphi),$$
where
$$p^{[0,\varphi]} = 1.$$
As a consequence
$$p^{[1,\varphi]} = p.$$

We can extend the definition of the generalized ascending factorial to the case where the first argument in brackets is negative: if $r > 0$, r integer, $\varphi > 0$, $\varphi \neq p, \frac{p}{2}, \ldots, \frac{p}{r}$, then

$$p^{[-r,\varphi]} = \frac{p}{p^{[r+1,-\varphi]}}.$$

The justification for this definition is found in Appendix 1.

It is also possible to have $k < 0$. With $k = -1$ we simply get sampling without replacement, and therefore hypergeometric distribution.

For values of φ negative or approaching zero, the distribution is unimodal, very similar to that of the binomial distribution. As φ increases the appearance of a bimodal form becomes more and more evident. It is easy to check that with $p = q = \varphi = 1/2$ we get uniform distribution on the integers $0, 1, \ldots, n$.

With $\varphi > 0$ it can be shown that, conditionally on θ, S_n is distributed as a binomial variable with parameters n and θ, that is

$$S_n|\theta \sim \mathcal{B}(n,\theta), \tag{1}$$

where θ possesses a beta distribution

$$\theta \sim \mathcal{B}(\gamma, \delta),$$

where

$$\gamma = \frac{p}{\varphi}, \qquad \delta = \frac{q}{\varphi}.$$

For this reason, in this context, S_n is also said to possess a betabinomial distribution. For future reference here are the factorial moments of θ ($h, k \geq 0$):

$$\begin{aligned}
\mathbf{E}[\theta^k(1-\theta)^h] &= \tag{2} \\
&= \frac{p(p+\varphi)(p+2\varphi)\cdots(p+(k-1)\varphi)q(q+\varphi)\cdots(q+(h-1)\varphi)}{(1+\varphi)(1+2\varphi)\cdots(1+(k+h-1)\varphi)} \\
&= \frac{p^{[k,\varphi]}q^{[h,\varphi]}}{1^{[k+h,\varphi]}}.
\end{aligned}$$

Because of the definition of the *incomplete beta function* the above formula (2) is still valid for negative powers of θ and $1-\theta$, subject to some restriction on the parameters. That is, if $h, k > 0$ and if

$$\varphi < \min\left(\frac{p}{k}, \frac{q}{h}\right),$$

then

$$\mathbf{E}[\theta^{-k}(1-\theta)^{-h}] = \frac{p^{[-k,\varphi]} q^{[-h,\varphi]}}{1^{[-k-h,\varphi]}} = \frac{pq 1^{[k+h+1,-\varphi]}}{p^{[k+1,-\varphi]} q^{[h+1,-\varphi]}}.$$

Consequently the central moments are given by

$$\mathbf{E}[\theta^k] = \frac{p^{[k,\varphi]}}{1^{[k,\varphi]}}.$$

It turns out that the $\{\alpha_i\}$ are conditionally independent given θ and are *exchangeable* (see *e.g.* Rényi (1970; p. 315)). It is easy to verify that

$$\mathbf{E}[\alpha_i] = p, \quad \mathbf{V}ar[\alpha_i] = pq, \quad \mathbf{C}ov[\alpha_i, \alpha_j] = \frac{pq\varphi}{1+\varphi},$$

so that

$$\mathbf{E}[S_n] = np, \quad \mathbf{V}ar[S_n] = npq + n(n-1)pq\rho,$$

where

$$\rho = \frac{\varphi}{1+\varphi}$$

is the correlation between α_i and α_j. To fully exploit the conditional distribution of S_n we are going to assume $\varphi > 0$. In this way ρ is an increasing function of φ and we can then think of φ as a measure of the dependence among the $\{\alpha_i\}$. With $\varphi \to 0$ we see binomial distribution and therefore independence.

Now let α_i be the indicator of the event that the i-th member accepts the project, and p be the probability of this event. So p represents individual precision or skill. Then $\varphi > 0$ can be thought of as a measure of the dependence among the members. Let S_n be defined as before.

Now consider the case of a polyarchy. The probability that a polyarchy accepts the project is given by

$$P_A = 1 - \mathbf{Pr}[S_n = 0].$$

With independence we have

$$P_{A_I} = 1 - (1-p)^n,$$

while with dependence

$$P_{A_D} = 1 - \mathbf{E}[(1-\theta)^n],$$

where

$$1 - \theta \sim \mathcal{B}(\delta, \gamma),$$

as defined above. Using (2) we get

$$\mathbf{E}[(1-\theta)^n] =$$
$$= \frac{(1-p)(1-p+\varphi)(1-p+2\varphi)\cdots(1-p+(n-1)\varphi)}{(1+\varphi)(1+2\varphi)\cdots(1+(n-1)\varphi)}.$$

Now we are going to prove a general result which allows the comparison of the previous relations. That is, we are going to prove

$$\frac{q(q+\varphi)(q+2\varphi)\cdots(q+(i-1)\varphi)}{(1+\varphi)(1+2\varphi)\cdots(1+(i-1)\varphi)} > q^i, \qquad i = 2, 3, \ldots \quad (3)$$

We are going to prove the above relationship by induction on m. Clearly the inequality is true for $m = 2$ since

$$\frac{q^2 + q\varphi}{1+\varphi} > q^2,$$

given our assumption $\varphi > 0$.

Let us assume that the inequality holds for $m > 2$. That is

$$B_m = \frac{q(q+\varphi)(q+2\varphi)\cdots(q+m\varphi)}{(1+\varphi)(1+2\varphi)\cdots(1+m\varphi)} > q^{m+1}.$$

Then we have to prove that

$$B_{m+1} = \frac{q(q+\varphi)(q+2\varphi)\cdots(q+(m+1)\varphi)}{(1+\varphi)(1+2\varphi)\cdots(1+(m+1)\varphi)} > q^{m+2}.$$

We can write

$$B_{m+1} = B_m \frac{q+(m+1)\varphi}{1+(m+1)\varphi}.$$

Now

$$\frac{q+(m+1)\varphi}{1+(m+1)\varphi} > q,$$

and then

$$B_{m+1} > B_m q > q^{m+2},$$

as we wanted.

Using this result we have

$$\mathbf{E}[(1-\theta)^n] > q^n,$$

and so

$$P_{A_I} > P_{A_D}.$$

Now consider the expected number of evaluations a project must undergo. Let us call this number of evaluations N_I and N_D respectively for the model with independence and for the model with dependence. Generally the number of evaluations can be written as

$$N = 1 + \tau_1(\psi),$$

where $\tau_1(\psi)$ is the waiting time of the first success in Bernoulli trials with success probability ψ, stopped at time $n-1$, that is

$$\mathbf{Pr}[\tau_1(\psi) = k] = \psi(1-\psi)^k, \qquad 0 \le k \le n-2,$$
$$\mathbf{Pr}[\tau_1(\psi) = n-1] = (1-\psi)^{n-1}.$$

Then

$$\mathbf{E}[N_I] = \frac{1-q^n}{1-q} = 1 + q + \ldots + q^{n-1}, \qquad (4)$$

where $q = 1 - p$. Again exploiting the conditional distribution (2) we have

$$\mathbf{E}[N_D] = \mathbf{E}\left[\frac{1-(1-\theta)^n}{1-\theta}\right] = 1 + \sum_{k=1}^{n-1} \mathbf{E}[(1-\theta)^k].$$

Using (2) the result is

$$\mathbf{E}[N_D] = 1 + \sum_{k=1}^{n-1} \frac{q^{[k,\varphi]}}{1^{[k,\varphi]}} \tag{5}.$$

Now applying (3) to each term of the series (4) and (5) we get

$$\mathbf{E}[N_D] > \mathbf{E}[N_I]. \tag{6}$$

Let us turn to the case of a hierarchy. The probability that a hierarchy accepts the project is given by

$$P_A = \mathbf{Pr}[S_n = n].$$

With independence we have

$$P^\star_{A_I} = p^n,$$

while with dependence

$$P^\star_{A_D} = \mathbf{E}[\theta^n].$$

Now

$$\mathbf{E}[\theta^n] = \frac{p(p+\varphi)(p+2\varphi)\cdots(p+(n-1)\varphi)}{(1+\varphi)(1+2\varphi)\cdots(1+(n-1)\varphi)}.$$

Replacing q with p in equation (3) we get

$$\frac{p(p+\varphi)(p+2\varphi)\cdots(p+(n-1)\varphi)}{(1+\varphi)(1+2\varphi)\cdots(1+(n-1)\varphi)} > p^n, \qquad n = 2, 3, \ldots \tag{7}$$

Then

$$\mathbf{E}[\theta^n] > p^n,$$

and consequently
$$P^{\star}_{A_I} < P^{\star}_{A_D}.$$

Let us now turn to the expected number of evaluations. With independence

$$\mathbf{E}[N^{\star}_I] = \frac{1-p^n}{1-p} = 1 + p + \ldots + p^{n-1}. \qquad (8)$$

In the case of dependence

$$\mathbf{E}[N^{\star}_D] = \mathbf{E}\left[\frac{1-\theta^n}{1-\theta}\right] = 1 + \sum_{k=1}^{n-1} \mathbf{E}[\theta^k].$$

Again using (2) we get

$$\mathbf{E}[N^{\star}_D] = 1 + \sum_{k=1}^{n-1} \frac{p^{[k,\varphi]}}{1^{[k,\varphi]}} \qquad (9).$$

Using (7) we can conclude

$$\mathbf{E}[N^{\star}_D] > \mathbf{E}[N^{\star}_I]. \qquad (10)$$

PART II

PYRAMID DECISION STRUCTURES

CHAPTER I

PYRAMIDAL STRUCTURES: A PRELIMINARY NOTE †

1. Introduction

We start with the consideration that human decisions are fallible. Let us consider an entrepreneur (if you prefer an owner, a dictator, etc.) who because of his information asymmetry or because of his lack of skills must rely on his collaborators in order to make a decision. To be more specific let the decision consist in accepting or rejecting a project drawn from a project portfolio. Within the portfolio there is a proportion π of good projects. Accepting a good project entails a benefit, while accepting a bad one entails a loss. The entrepreneur has N collaborators, each of whom is identical and independent in the decision making process. Each collaborator has a probability p_1 to accept a good project and a

---

† Reprinted, with slight modifications, from *Riv. Inter. di Scienze Economiche e Commerciali*, 6-7, 1993.

probability p_2 to accept a bad one: hence $(1-p_1)$ is the probability of an error of the first type, and p_2 is the probability of an error of the second type.

The different decision structures (i.e. rules determining the decision process) must somehow be compared in terms of performance measured, for example, by the resulting expected net benefit.

The economic literature (Bull and Ordover, 1987; Miller, 1992; Sah, 1991; Sah and Stiglitz, 1985, 1986, 1988a, 1988b) has traditionally considered three kinds of decision structures: hierarchy, polyarchy and committee. Hierarchy is defined as the structure that accepts a project if and only if all of its members have accepted it. Polyarchy is a structure such that if one member accepts a project this project is definitively accepted by the structure. If, on the other hand, the project is rejected it may be evaluated by another member who ignores the precedent rejection. If the project succeeds in passing this second evaluation it will be definitively accepted. And so on. This scheme is probabilistically equivalent to a model where the rule of acceptance is to accept if at least one member accepts. The committee is a structure where the members decide jointly and simultaneously. The decision is made according to a consensus rule k, where $0 < k < N$. That means that the structure accepts a project if at least k members accept it. As far as the consensus level is concerned, we can consider hierarchy and polyarchy as committees whose consensus level is $k = N$ and $k = 1$ respectively.

If, on the other hand, a cost is attached to each evaluation, there is a substantial difference between a committee and hierarchy or polyarchy, since in the committee the decision is made simultaneously, while in the other two structures it is made sequentially. In order to assess the functioning cost of each structure, an important variable to be considered may be the expected number of evaluations of each project. The expected number for a committee acting simultaneously might be considered equal to 1.

Let us assume that the project is good (analogous formulas interchanging p_1 with p_2 hold in the case of a bad project).

In the case of hierarchy, the expected number of evaluations is

$$\sum_{i=1}^{N-1} i(1-p_1)p_1^{i-1} + Np_1^{N-1}.$$

In the case of polyarchy we have

$$\sum_{i=1}^{N-1} ip_1(1-p_1)^{i-1} + N(1-p_1)^{N-1}.$$

Let us note that with this approach, hierarchy turns out to be a decision structure with N levels each of which is composed of the same number of members equal to 1. This configuration appears to be a restrictive description of a hierarchy, at least as far as the notion is conventionally conceived: the traditional hierarchy represents a pyramid configuration with a large bottom and a slim top. Given N and the number of levels k we can have many pyramid configurations. The first goal of this chapter is to rank these configurations, in what can be interpreted as a sort of a genetic development of hierarchy. Then the consistency of this ordering with the ordering of some variables characterising the decision process (the probability to accept a good project, or the expected number of evaluations) can be ascertained.

4. Hierarchy as a pyramid configuration

We consider here the subdivision of N individuals into k levels, referred to as subcommittees. We examine only pyramid structures, that is structures characterised by a series of levels each of which consists of a number of elements (members) not greater than that of the level immediately below. In this structure we introduce a *quasi-lexicographic* ordering of configurations which can be considered as a law of evolution from an *originary* configuration. From a dynamic point of view, this ordering can be stated as follows: from each configuration the next one is obtained through a movement of one unit from the bottom level to that immediately above (the second level), while maintaining a pyramid configuration. If it is not possible, it is obtained through a movement of one unit from the second level to the third one, again maintaining a pyramid configuration, if it is possible ... and so on.

We define the *originary* configuration as the configuration having $(N - k + 1)$ elements at the bottom level and one element in all of the other $(k - 1)$ levels.

In this quasi-lexicographic ordering, the following property holds when you move ahead in the dictionary: if the bottom level remains constant then the top level increases (that is the number of the elements of this level increases); if the top level remains constant, then the bottom level decreases. The bottom level never increases.

A formula is stated in the Appendix which gives the number of configurations generated according to this law, for any N and k.

The following are rules governing the decision process of each configuration:

1) each subcommittee behaves as a polyarchy; thus, a project is accepted if and only if at least one of its members accepts it;

2) among themselves the subcommittees behave as a hierarchy (in the meaning of Sah and Stiglitz); that is the structure accepts a project if and only if all the subcommittees have accepted it.

In the Appendix we prove the following result.

Let $k = 3$ and let $\mathcal{P}_1$ ($\mathcal{P}_2$) denote the probability that a configuration (given N and k) accepts a good project (or accepts a bad project). Then our quasi-lexicographic ordering is consistent with an ordering of $\mathcal{P}_1$ ($\mathcal{P}_2$) in so far as that for each value of p_1 (p_2) (that is the individual probability to accept a good (bad) project), $\mathcal{P}_1$ ($\mathcal{P}_2$) increases monotonically, moving ahead in the dictionary.

Another result obtained in the Appendix is the following.

For simplicity let us assume $p_2 = 0$. The Appendix shows how to calculate the expected number of evaluations of each configuration corresponding to any N and k. For each configuration the expected number of evaluations is a function of p_1. Let us consider for each p_1 the configuration for which the expected number of evaluations is maximum. In the Appendix we consider the configurations which result when $N = 10$ and $k = 3$. We can see that, increasing p_1 from 0 to 1, the configuration presenting the maximum moves ahead in the dictionary (see Fig. 1 in the Appendix).

With $p_2 = 0$, the only cost that can arise from the decision made is that relative to the rejection of a good project. Consequently this potential cost is minimised when the probability ($\mathcal{P}_1$) to accept a good project is maximised. On the other hand the expected number of evaluations can be taken as a measure of the cost of the decision process. The greater this number is, the costlier the decision process is. In general, depending on the relative values of these two types of costs, we can determine the configuration that allows the minimum cost (the optimal configuration).

In our example it is possible to say something more.

Using the obtained results, if p_1 is sufficiently close to 0, then doubtlessly the optimal configuration is the last one in the dictionary (since this configuration permits the greatest value of $\mathcal{P}_1$ and the lowest value of the expected number of evaluations).

For values of p_1 sufficiently greater than 1/2 the optimal configuration is found among the last ones in the dictionary.

3. Conclusions

In this chapter we have introduced a quasi-lexicographic ordering of the pyramid decision structures. This ordering can be depicted as a particular *evolution law*. This ordering turned out to be consistent with $\mathcal{P}_1$ (the probability to accept a good project) and $\mathcal{P}_2$ (the probability to reject a bad project). Even the expected number of evaluations, in some respects, is consistently ordered.

The obtained results can be a good starting point for modelling the dynamics of the decision structures.

The *evolution law* can be understood as the result of the interaction between the members' goal to be promoted (to move from one level of the configuration to the upper one), and the economic and strategic calculus of the entrepreneur.

Appendix

With the *quasi-lexicographic* ordering previously defined, here we give the formula that allows us to calculate the number $\mu(N, k)$ of different configurations (composition of the subcommittees) in the case of N members to be subdivided in k levels (subcommittees). This formula has not been obtained analytically, but has been derived through study of the regularities of the actual values for different N and k, and then checked for many values of N and k.

First of all, N must be greater or equal to k, and for

$$\begin{aligned} N &= k, & \mu &= 1, \\ N &= k+1, & \mu &= 1, \\ N &= k+2, & \mu &= 2, \\ N &= k+3, & \mu &= 2. \end{aligned}$$

The following symbols will be used.

Let us subdivide all the numbers $N > k+3$ in groups "h", $h = 1, 2, \ldots$

For $h \leq k-2$, the numbers N belonging to group h are those such that

$$k + \sum_{i=1}^{h+1} i + 1 \leq N \leq k + \sum_{i=1}^{h+2} i,$$

while for $h > k-2$ the groups are defined by

$$(h-k+2)k + \sum_{i=1}^{k} i + 1 \leq N \leq (h-k+2)k + k + \sum_{i=1}^{k} i.$$

So, given N and k, the group h which N belongs to is determined. Now with $h \leq k-2$, let

$$\varphi_h = \varphi_{h-1} + \sum_{i=1}^{h+1},$$

with $\varphi_0 = 2$.
Then

$$\varphi_h = 2 + \sum_{j=2}^{h+1} \sum_{i=1}^{j} i$$

$$= 1 + \frac{(h+1)(h+2)(2h+6)}{12}.$$

If $h > k-2$, the analogous formula is

$$\varphi_h = 1 + \frac{(k-1)k(2k+2)}{12} + \frac{(h-k+2)(k-1)}{2}.$$

Now let π_{1h} be the value corresponding to the first element of group h:

$$\pi_{1h} = \begin{cases} h+1, & \text{if } h \le k-2, \\ k-1, & \text{if } h > k-2 \end{cases}$$

Let π_{2h} be the value corresponding to the second element of group h; then

$$\pi_{2h} = \pi_{1h} - 1.$$

And so on for π_{ih}. Now let ν_h be the number of elements in group h; then

$$\nu_h = \pi_{1h} + 1.$$

Finally let n_h be the position of N (which belongs to group h) in the group h:

$$n_h = 1, 2, \ldots, \nu_h.$$

Then the number of configurations $\mu(N, k)$ is given by

$$\mu(N, k) = \varphi_{h-1} + \sum_{i=1}^{n_h} \pi_{ih}.$$

For example with $N = 10$ and $k = 3$, it turns out that $h = 2$, so $\varphi_{h-1} = \varphi_1 = 1 + 48/12 = 5$,

$$n_h = n_2 = 1,$$

$$\pi_{1h} = \pi_{12} = 2,$$

$$\sum_{i=1}^{n_h} \pi_{ih} = \sum_{i=1}^{1} \pi_{i2} = 2.$$

Consequently

$$\mu(10, 3) = 5 + 2 = 7,$$

and the ordered configurations are

$$\begin{array}{ccc} 8, & 1, & 1 \\ 7, & 2, & 1 \\ 6, & 3, & 1 \\ 5, & 4, & 1 \\ 5, & 3, & 2 \\ 4, & 4, & 2 \\ 4, & 3, & 3 \end{array}$$

In any triple, the first number represents the first (bottom) level, the second number the second level and the third number the third (top) level. (8, 1, 1) plays the role of the *originary* configuration.

In the defined ordering the following property holds: when moving ahead in the ordering, if the bottom level is constant the top level increases; if the top level is constant the bottom level decreases; furthermore the bottom level never increases.

Let us restate here the assumptions concerning the operating mode of our decision structure:

1) each member has the same probability to accept a good project (say p_1) and the same probability to accept a bad project (say p_2); furthermore each member is independent.

2) each level (subcommittee) behaves as a polyarchy, that is, a project is accepted if and only if at least one member accepts it.

3) the subcommittees behave among themselves as a hierarchy, that is, the structure accepts a project if and only if all the subcommittees have accepted it.

To simplify, let us write p for the probability of accepting a project (or p_1 if the project is good and p_2 if the project is bad).

Let $\mathcal{P}$ be the probability that the structure accepts a project. Let n_i, $i = 1, 2, \ldots, k$, be the number of elements in the i-th subcommittee starting from and including the bottom:

$$n_1 \geq n_2 \geq \ldots \geq n_k, \qquad \sum_{i=1}^{k} n_i = N,$$

and furthermore obeying the stated rules of pyramid structures.

Given our assumptions, we get

$$\mathcal{P} = [1 - (1-p)^{n_1}][1 - (1-p)^{n_2}] \times \ldots \times [1 - (1-p)^{n_k}].$$

Let $k = 3$.

Now we are going to prove that our *quasi-lexicographic* ordering is consistent with an ordering of $\mathcal{P}$; more precisely moving ahead in the ordering, $\mathcal{P}$ monotonically increases.

Let x stand for n_1, y for n_3 and $N - x - y$ for n_2. Using the above mentioned property, when y is constant x decreases and when x is constant y increases.

Treating x and y as continuous variables, we calculate the partial derivative of $\mathcal{P}$ with respect to x while keeping y constant, and then the partial derivative of $\mathcal{P}$ with respect to y while keeping x constant. We get

$$\frac{\partial \mathcal{P}}{\partial x} = \log(1-p)[1-(1-p)^y][(1-p)^{N-x-y} - (1-p)^x].$$

Since

$$x \geq N - x - y \geq y,$$

it follows that

$$\frac{\partial \mathcal{P}}{\partial x} < 0.$$

Analogously

$$\frac{\partial \mathcal{P}}{\partial y} = \log(1-p)[1-(1-p)^x][(1-p)^{N-x-y} - (1-p)^y],$$

and so

$$\frac{\partial \mathcal{P}}{\partial y} > 0.$$

Using the above mentioned property this yields the desired result.

Now let $m(N, k, \omega)$ be the number of evaluations that a project has to pass before a decision is reached by the structure, relative to a pyramid with N members, k levels, and configuration ω. ω is identified by the set of k numbers $\{n_1, n_2, \ldots, n_k\}$.

At this stage we are concerned with the expected value of this number of evaluations, to be denoted by $\mathbf{E}[m(N, k, \omega)]$.

This turns out to be a particular and more complicated case of waiting times.

Let us assume that the project is good; and therefore that p stands for p_1. Let k be arbitrary.

In the case of a polyarchy with n members, let $t(n)$ be the waiting time of the acceptance of a project: $t(n) = \infty$ if the project is rejected. Furthermore let $\tau(n)$ be the number of evaluations a project has to pass before a decision is made:

$$\tau(n) = \begin{cases} t(n) + 1, & \text{if} \quad t(n) < \infty, \\ n, & \text{if} \quad t(n) = \infty. \end{cases}$$

Then the expected number of evaluations is given by

$$\mathbf{E}[\tau(n)] = p \sum_{i=1}^{N-1} i(1-p)^{i-1} + N(1-p)^{N-1}. \tag{1}$$

Now let $t_i(n)$ and $\tau_i(n)$ be the analogous variables referring to the i-th level from, and including, the bottom.

Let us define the random variables $\chi_1, \chi_2, \ldots, \chi_k$ in the following way: χ_1 is the number of evaluations occurring in the bottom level, that is

$$\chi_1 = \tau_1(n_1);$$

$$\chi_2 = \begin{cases} 0, & \text{if} \quad t_1(n_1) = \infty, \\ \tau_2(n_2), & \text{if} \quad t_1(n_1) < \infty; \end{cases}$$

$$\cdots \quad \cdots \quad \cdots$$

$$\chi_j =$$

$$= \begin{cases} 0, & \text{if} \quad t_1 = \infty \vee t_1 < \infty, t_2 = \infty \vee \ldots \\ & \vee t_1 < \infty, t_2 < \infty, \ldots, t_{j-1} = \infty, \\ \tau_j, & \text{if} \quad t_1 < \infty, t_2 < \infty, \vee, t_{j-1} < \infty, \end{cases}$$

where τ_j is a short form of $\tau_j(n_j)$.
Now

$$m(N, k, \omega) = \sum_{i=1}^{k} \chi_i,$$

and

$$\mathbf{E}[m(N, k, \omega)] = \sum_{i=1}^{k} \mathbf{E}[\chi_i].$$

Now we have

$$\mathbf{E}[\chi_1] = \mathbf{E}[\tau_1(n_1)],$$
$$\mathbf{E}[\chi_i] = \mathbf{E}[\tau_i(n_i)]\mathbf{Pr}[t_1 < \infty, t_2 < \infty, \ldots, t_{i-1} < \infty],$$

where

$$\mathbf{Pr}[t_1 < \infty, t_2 < \infty, \ldots, t_{i-1} < \infty] =$$
$$= [1 - (1-p)^{n_1}][1 - (1-p)^{n_2}] \times \ldots \times [1 - (1-p)^{n_{i-1}}],$$

and

$$\mathbf{E}[\tau_i(n_i)]$$

is given by the formula (1).

In Figure 1 we depict the expected value of the number of evaluations as a function of p in the case $N = 10$ and $k = 3$: each triple $\{n_1, n_2, n_3\}$ identifies an ω. If, for simplicity, $p_2 = 0$, the unconditional expected value (that is, regardless of whether the project is good or bad) is obtained simply by adding 1 to each curve appearing in the figure.

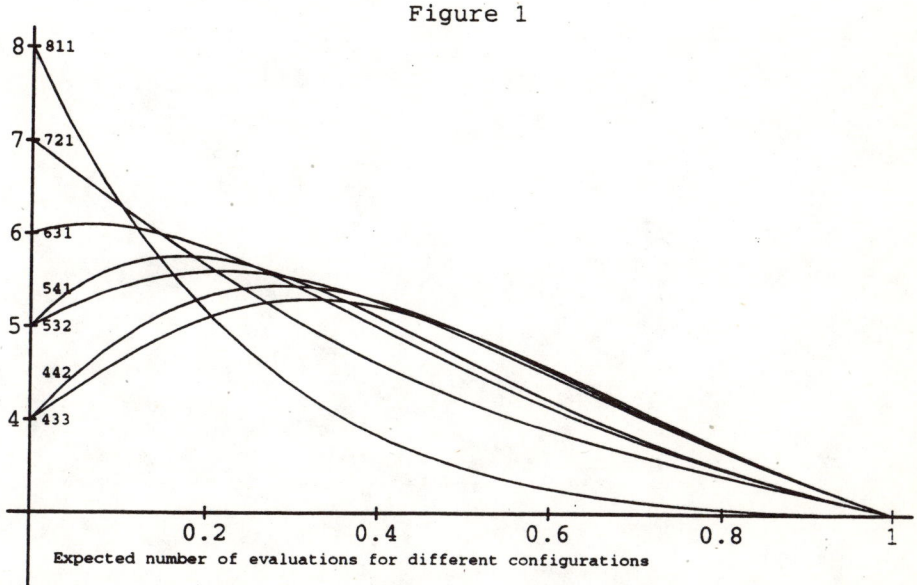

Figure 1

Expected number of evaluations for different configurations

CHAPTER II

OTHER PROPERTIES OF PYRAMIDS

1. Introduction

In the previous chapter we defined a decision structure, called a pyramid decision structure, which is composed of a series of levels consisting of a number of elements not greater than that of the level immediately below. If the decision to be made is of a dichotomous type, for example whether to accept or to reject a project, then each level behaves as a polyarchy, that is the level accepts the project if at least one of its members accepts it. Furthermore the levels as a whole act as a hierarchy, that is the whole structure accepts the project if all the levels accept it. As a matter of convention, let the *bottom level* be that with the most elements and the *top level* that with the fewest. Given N, the total number of components of the structure, and k, the number of levels, we have different possible configurations of the pyramid, depending on the distribution of the members across levels. We introduced a *quasi-lexicographic* ordering of configurations which was considered a sort of law of evolution from an originary configuration. The *originary* configuration is characterised as containing just one element, per level, with the exception of the bottom level. The "law of evolution" can thus be stated in the following way: from each configuration the next one is obtained through a movement of one unit from the bottom level to that immediately above, if it is possible to do so and to maintain a pyramid configuration. If it is not, the next configuration is derived through a movement of one unit from the second level to the third one, if it is possible ... and so on. We start from the originary configuration and when we reach a configuration that does not allow further movement we say that the structure has reached the *stable* configuration. In this quasi-lexicographic ordering, each configuration is situated in a "dictionary" where the first *word* is the originary configuration and the last word is the stable configuration. To make things clearer we formalize in this way. A *configuration* of the pyramid, given N and k, to be indicated with $\omega(N,k)$, is a set of k numbers: $\{n_1, n_2, \ldots, n_k\}$, such that

$$\sum_{i=1}^{k} n_i = N, \qquad n_1 \geq n_2 \geq \ldots \geq n_k. \tag{1}$$

That is to say, the first number of the set is the number of elements of the bottom level, the last one that of the elements of the top level, and generally the i-th number is the number of elements of the i-th level, $1 \leq i \leq k$. The originary configuration is

$$\omega_o(N,k) = \{N-k+1, 1, \ldots, 1, 1\}.$$

2. A new recursive formula for the number of configurations

In Chapter I of Part II a formula was given to calculate the number of resulting configurations, given N and k. Let us call this number $\nu(N,k)$. Here we give a new formula, in a recursive form,

which is more readily understood. Let us say that the numbers N are *regular* if
$$N \geq \frac{k(k+1)}{2} + 1.$$

Given k and a regular N, let us define the non-negative integer m in such a way as to satisfy

$$mk + 1 + \frac{k(k+1)}{2} \leq N \leq (m+1)k + \frac{k(k+1)}{2}, \qquad m \geq 0.$$

Let us define

$$\delta = N - mk - 1 - \frac{k(k+1)}{2}, \qquad \delta = 0, 1, \ldots, k-1.$$

Then

$$\nu(N+1, k) = \begin{cases} \nu(N, k) + k - 2 - \delta, & \text{if } \delta \leq k-2 \\ \nu(N, k) + k - 1, & \text{if } \delta = k-1, \end{cases}$$

with

$$\nu(N_m, k) = \varphi_k + k - 1,$$

where N_m is the minimum value of N at regimen, that is

$$N_m = 1 + \frac{k(k+1)}{2},$$

and

$$\varphi_k = 1 + \frac{2k(k-1)(k-2)}{12}.$$

3. A formula for determining the stable configuration

Now we are going to establish the formula that allows the stable configuration $\omega_s(N, k)$ to be written when we start with the originary configuration and follow the evolution described above. If

$$N = \frac{k(k+1)}{2},$$

we say that

$$\omega_s(N, k) = \{k, k-1, k-2, \ldots, 3, 2, 1\}. \qquad (\star)$$

The reasons for this result follow. First of all, since this is a stable configuration, each two adjoining levels must differ at most by one element. Secondly, each configuration cannot contain more than one couple of adjoining levels with the same composition (unless the other couple is made out of ones); by the same token, each configuration cannot contain a triple of adjoining levels with the same composition, and so on. It "cannot contain" means that such a configuration cannot be found in the "dictionary". To demonstrate this let us assume that indeed there exists such a configuration, for example a configuration with two couples of adjoining levels with the same composition (and none of them made out of ones). Then we should be able to move back in the dictionary to trace the genetic history of this configuration. What really happens is that we find a non-pyramidal ancestor of this configuration. For example, let the configuration be $\{5, 5, 4, 3, 2, 2\}$. Then moving back a step at a time we might have this sequence: $\{6, 4, 4, 3, 2, 2\}$, $\{6, 5, 3, 3, 2, 2\}$, $\{7, 4, 3, 3, 2, 2\}$, $\{8, 3, 3, 3, 2, 2\}$, and finally $\{9, 2, 3, 3, 2, 2\}$, which is not a pyramid. It follows that the configuration $(\star)$ is necessarily the stable configuration.

Now suppose that

$$N = \frac{k(k+1)}{2} + 1.$$

Then the same reasoning as before allows us to conclude that

$$\omega_s(N, k) = \{k, k-1, k-2, \ldots, 3, 2, 2\}.$$

Continuing in this way we obtain the general formula. Let

$$N - \frac{k(k+1)}{2} = \mu, \qquad \mu \geq 0.$$

Clearly, μ is an integer. We can thus write

$$\mu = rk + s, \qquad s < k, \qquad r = 0, 1, \ldots$$

The stable configuration can be written in this way

$$\omega_s(N,k) = \{k+r, k+r-1, \ldots, r+s+2, r+s+1,$$
$$r+s+1, r+s, \ldots, 4+r, 3+r, 2+r\},$$

where the couple with identical values $r+s+1$ corresponds to the levels s-th and $(s+1)$-st descending from the top level, that is going backward from the last element of the previous list. It is just slightly more complicated to derive the formula in the case of $\mu < 0$. If it is so, then we can determine i in such a way that

$$ik - \frac{i(i+1)}{2} < \frac{k(k+1)}{2} - N \leq (i+1)k - \frac{(i+1)(i+2)}{2},$$

where $i = 0, 1, \ldots, k-2$. Let us call $i^\star$ the value of i so determined. Let us put

$$\frac{k(k+1)}{2} - N - i^\star k + \frac{i^\star(i^\star+1)}{2} = t.$$

Then we have

$$\omega_s(N,k) = \{k - i^\star - 1, k - i^\star - 2, k - i^\star - 3, \ldots, k - i^\star - t,$$
$$k - i^\star - t, k - i^\star - t - 1, \ldots, 1, 1\},$$

where the couple having the same value $k - i^\star + 1 - t$ corresponds to the levels t-eth and $(t+1)$-st ascending from the bottom level, that is moving forward from the first element of the previous list, while the string of ones begins at the $(i^\star + 1)$-st level starting from the last element.

4. The probability of accepting a good project

We make the following assumptions about individual behavior. All the members possess the same probability p of making the right decision, and they make their decision independently of the others. To simplify matters, let us assume that the project under scrutiny is good. Then p is the individual probability to accept the project. In Chapter I of Part II it was proved that, with $N = 10$

and $k = 3$, the quasi-lexicographic ordering of configurations was consistent with an increasing ordering of the probabilities of accepting the project. In other words it corresponded to an increase in the probability of accepting a project while moving ahead in the dictionary of configurations. Here we are going to generalize this result for arbitrary values of N and k. The evolution law from the originary configuration, as described, means that we have the sequence

(1) n_1 decreases, n_2 increases, n_3 is constant, ..., n_k is constant,

(2) n_1 is constant, n_2 decreases, n_3 increases, ..., n_k is constant,

(3) n_1 is constant, n_2 is constant, n_3 decreases, ..., n_k is constant,

. . . . . .

again (1), (2), (3), ..., until reaching the stable configuration.

Remark. The last configuration of each group is the first of the following group.

Let us consider any two consecutive configurations of group (1). Let P_{11} and P_{21} be the corresponding probabilities. Then, for some r,

$$P_{11} = (1 - q^{n_1-r})(1 - q^{n_2+r})(1 - q^{n_3}) \cdots (1 - q^{n_k}),$$

$$P_{21} = (1 - q^{n_1-r-1})(1 - q^{n_2+r+1})(1 - q^{n_3}) \cdots (1 - q^{n_k}).$$

Then, using the result given in Appendix 1,

$$(1 - q^{n_1-r})(1 - q^{n_2+r}) < (1 - q^{n_1-r-1})(1 - q^{n_2+r+1}),$$

and so

$$P_{11} < P_{21}.$$

Now let us consider any two consecutive configurations of group (2). Let P_{12} and P_{22} be the corresponding probabilities. Then, for some r_1, r_2, r_3,

$$P_{12} = (1 - q^{n_1-r_1})(1 - q^{n_2+r_2})(1 - q^{n_3+r_3}) \cdots (1 - q^{n_k}),$$

$$P_{22} = (1 - q^{n_1-r_1})(1 - q^{n_2+r_2-1})(1 - q^{n_3+r_3+1}) \cdots (1 - q^{n_k}).$$

Then, using again the result in Appendix 1,

$$(1 - q^{n_2+r_2})(1 - q^{n_3+r_3}) < (1 - q^{n_2+r_2-1})(1 - q^{n_3+r_3+1}),$$

and so

$$P_{12} < P_{22}.$$

Repeating the same argument for all the groups and applying the *Remark*, we can conclude that probability strictly increases as we move ahead in the dictionary.

5. The expected number of evaluations

Now we are going to evaluate the expected number of evaluations in a polyarchy with n members, given that the polyarchy has accepted the project. Let A denote the event "the polyarchy accepts the project" and let $q = 1 - p$. Then

$$\mathbf{Pr}[\tau_P = h | A] = \frac{pq^{h-1}}{1 - q^n} \qquad h = 1, \ldots, n.$$

Now

$$E[\tau_P | A] = \frac{p}{1 - q^n} \sum_{h=1}^{n} h q^{h-1}.$$

Since

$$\sum_{h=1}^{n} h q^{h-1} = \frac{1 - (n+1)q^n + n q^{n+1}}{(1 - q)^2},$$

we get

$$E[\tau_P | A] = \frac{1 - (n+1)q^n + n q^{n+1}}{(1 - q)(1 - q^n)}.$$

In Appendix 2 it is shown that

$$E[\tau_P | A] < E[\tau_P].$$

Now let us turn to our pyramid structures. We want to provide a formula to calculate the expected number of evaluations in a pyramid with N members and k levels. As usual

$$n_1 \geq n_2 \geq \ldots \geq n_k.$$

Let T be the number of evaluations of the structure. Let us denote with τ_i the number of evaluations at level i. Furthermore, let A_i denote the event "the i-th level accepts the project", and A_i^c the event "the i-th level does not accept the project". Then

$$E[T] = E[\tau_1|A_1^c] \cdot Pr[A_1^c] + [E[\tau_1|A_1] + E[\tau_2|A_2^c]] \cdot Pr[A_1, A_1^c]$$
$$+ [E[\tau_1|A_1] + E[\tau_2|A_2] + E[\tau_3|A_3^c]] \cdot Pr[A_1, A_2, A_3^c]$$
$$+ \ldots$$
$$+ [E[\tau_1|A_1] + \ldots + E[\tau_{k-1}|A_{k-1}] + E[\tau_k]] \times$$
$$\times Pr[A_1, A_2, \ldots, A_{k-1}].$$

Using independence among levels, rearranging the terms and using properties of the conditional expected value, this expression can be simplified to

$$E[T] = E[\tau_1] + E[\tau_2] \cdot Pr[A_1] + E[\tau_3] \cdot Pr[A_1] \cdot P[A_2] + \ldots$$
$$+ E[\tau_k] \cdot Pr[A_1] \cdot Pr[A_2] \cdots Pr[A_{k-1}],$$

where

$$E[\tau_i] = \frac{1 - q^{n_i}}{1 - q}, \qquad \mathbf{Pr}[A_i] = 1 - q^{n_i}.$$

6. Different k for the same N

Let N be of the type $\frac{h(h+1)}{2}$, for some h. We want to confront the expected number of evaluations for different k when $k = 1$, which means polyarchy, when $k = N$, which means hierarchy, and when $k = h$, in which case we consider the stable configuration as given in Section 3. Let us denote with τ_S the number of evaluations in the case of this stable configuration. We are going to show that

$$E[\tau_S] > E[\tau_H] \quad if \quad p < \frac{1}{2},$$

$$E[\tau_S] > E[\tau_P] \quad if \quad p > \frac{1}{2}.$$

Using the results of the previous section we have

$$E[\tau_S] = \frac{1-q^h}{p} + \frac{1-q^{h-1}}{p}(1-q^h)$$
$$+ \frac{1-q^{h-2}}{p}(1-q^h)(1-q^{h-1}) + \cdots$$
$$+ (1-q^h)(1-q^{h-1})\cdots(1-q^2).$$

Let us start with the case $p < 1/2$. Then, using the result in Appendix 3 and the obvious fact that $q^h < q$, we have

$$E[\tau_S] \geq \frac{1-p^h}{q} + \frac{1-p^{h-1}}{q}(1-q^h)$$
$$+ \frac{1-p^{h-2}}{q}(1-q^h)(1-q^{h-1})$$
$$+ \cdots + (1-q^h)(1-q^{h-1})\cdots(1-q^2)$$
$$\geq \frac{1-p^h}{q} + \frac{1-p^{h-1}}{q}p + \frac{1-p^{h-2}}{q}p^2 + \cdots + p^{h-1}$$
$$= \frac{1}{q}[1 - p^h + (1-p^{h-1})p + (1-p^{h-2})p^2 + \cdots$$
$$+ (1-p)p^{h-1}]$$
$$= \frac{1}{q}\sum_{i=1}^{h}(1-p^i)p^{h-i}$$
$$\geq \frac{1}{q}(1-p^N)$$
$$= E[\tau_H],$$

where the last inequality is due to the first result given in the

Appendix 4. Now let us turn to the case $p > 1/2$.

$$E[\tau_S] \geq \frac{1-q^h}{p} + \frac{1-q^{h-1}}{p}p + \frac{1-q^{h-2}}{p}p^2 + \ldots + p^{h-1}$$

$$= \frac{1}{p}[1 - q^h + (1-q^{h-1})p + (1-q^{h-2})p^2 + \ldots$$

$$+ (1-q)p^{h-1}]$$

$$= \frac{1}{p}\sum_{i=1}^{h}(1-q^i)p^{h-i}$$

$$\geq \frac{1}{p}(1-q^N)$$

$$= E[\tau_P],$$

where the last inequality is due to second result given in Appendix 4.

Appendix 1

To prove, if $n_1 > n_2 + 1$,

$$\frac{1-q^{n_1-1}}{1-q^{n_2}} > \frac{1-q^{n_1}}{1-q^{n_2+1}}.$$

Proof

Let us consider the function

$$f(k) = \frac{1-q^{x+k}}{1-q^{y+k}} \qquad x > y, \quad 0 < q < 1.$$

The numerator of the derivative with respect to k, after dividing for q^k is equal to

$$\log q \left[(1-q^{x+k})q^y - (1-q^{y+k})q^x\right].$$

It follows that

$$\frac{\partial f(k)}{\partial k} < 0,$$

and this proves our assertion.

Appendix 2

First of all let us note that the quantity

$$q^n - nq + n - 1$$

strictly decreases in q. Consequently

$$1 - n + nq < q^n,$$
$$-(n+1) + nq < q^n - 2,$$
$$1 - (n+1)q^n + nq^{n+1} < q^{2n} - 2q^n + 1,$$
$$1 - (n+1)q^n + nq^{n+1} < (1 - q^n)^2,$$
$$\frac{1 - (n+1)q^n + nq^{n+1}}{1 - q^n} < 1 - q^n,$$
$$\frac{1 - (n+1)q^n + nq^{n+1}}{(1 - q^n)(1 - q)} < \frac{1 - q^n}{1 - q},$$

whence the desired result.

Appendix 3

Assume that the project is good. Let p be the probability to accept a good project, e.g. the probability to make the correct decision. Let τ_H denote the number of evaluations a project must undergo in the case of a hierarchy, and τ_P in the case of a polyarchy. Then the expected values are given by

$$E(\tau_H) = \frac{1 - p^N}{q},$$

$$E(\tau_P) = \frac{1 - q^N}{p},$$

where $q = 1 - p$. Comparing the two it is easy to see that

$$E[\tau_H] < E[\tau_P] \quad if \quad p < 1/2,$$

$$E[\tau_H] = E[\tau_P] \quad if \quad p = 1/2,$$
$$E[\tau_H] > E[\tau_P] \quad if \quad p > 1/2.$$

Appendix 4

We are going to prove that for $n > 1$, if $p < 1/2$

$$\sum_{i=1}^{n}(1-p^i)p^{n-i} \geq 1.$$

This is due the fact that

$$\sum_{i=1}^{n}(1-p^i)p^{n-i} = 1 + \sum_{i=1}^{n-1}p^{n-i} - np^n,$$

and

$$\sum_{i=1}^{n-1}p^{n-i} - np^n \geq \sum_{i=1}^{n-1}p^{n-i} - np^{n-1}$$
$$= \sum_{i=2}^{n-1}p^{n-i} - (n-1)p^{n-1}$$
$$\geq \sum_{i=2}^{n-1}p^{n-i} - (n-1)p^{n-2}$$
$$\cdots\cdots$$
$$\geq \sum_{i=n-1}^{n-1}p^{n-i} - (n-n+2)p^{n-n+2}$$
$$= p - 2p^2 \geq 0.$$

Consequently

$$\sum_{i=1}^{n}(1-p^i)p^{n-i} \geq 1 - p^{\frac{n(n+1)}{2}}. \qquad (1)$$

On the other hand, if $p > 1/2$, then $q = 1 - p < 1/2$ and so

$$\sum_{i=1}^{n}(1-q^i)q^{n-i} \geq 1 - q^{\frac{n(n+1)}{2}}.$$

Furthermore, since now $p > q$, we can conclude that

$$\sum_{i=1}^{n}(1-q^i)p^{n-i} \geq 1 - q^{\frac{n(n+1)}{2}}. \tag{2}$$

CHAPTER   III

PYRAMIDS AND DEPENDENCE

1. Introduction

In Chapters I and II of Part II the pyramid decision structure was analyzed and defined as having the following characteristics. The structure is composed of a series of levels each composed of a number of members not greater than that of the level immediately below. If the decision to be made is of a dichotomous type, for example accepting or rejecting a project, then each level behaves as a polyarchy, that is each level accepts the project if at least one of its members accepts it. Taken together, the levels act as a hierarchy, that is, the whole structure accepts a project if all the levels accept it. Each member shares the same probability p to make the right decision, and acts independently from all the other members.

Hierarchy and polyarchy were introduced by Sah and Stiglitz (for example 1985, 1986, 1988a, 1988b) and Sah (1991) as particular types of decision structures dealing with dichotomous choices. A polyarchy accepts a project when at least one of its members accepts it; a hierarchy accepts a project when all of its members accept it. For our purposes let us note here that probabilistically a polyarchy is equivalent to a sequence of individual evaluations of a project which stops should a first individual accepts the project. In contrast, a hierarchy is equivalent to a sequence of evaluations that stops when a first individual does not accept the project.

The object of this Chapter is to introduce some models of dependence among the different levels, while retaining the assumption of independence among the members of the same level. There are essentially three models of dependence. In the first one, the time spent to reach a decision depends on the time spent at the preceding level; in the second one the correctness of the decision made depends on the time spent at the preceding level; and in the last one the number of members of each level (apart from the first one, which is fixed) depends on the number of evaluations a project had to pass at the preceding level. We studied these models probabilistically, identifying the characterizing parameters. Also, in the case of the third model, an application is presented which shows how to determine the optimal number of members at the first level.

2. Making the intensity of the effort variable

In what follows we assume that the project under scrutiny is good. Consequently the right decision is to accept the project and p is the individual probability of doing so.

We consider a pyramid with two levels; the generalization to more levels is straightforward. Let n_1 be the number of members at the first level.

Let τ_1 be the individual time spent in reaching a decision for a member belonging to the first level. Furthermore, let T_1 be the total time spent at the first level in reaching a decision. We assume

$$\tau_1 \sim G(\alpha, 1), \qquad (1)$$

that is, τ_1 possesses a *Gamma distribution* with the stated parameters. The parameter α can be thought of as a measure of the loyalty of the members with respect to the structure. Loyalty governs the intensity of the effort devoted to the decision process, therefore loyalty is an increasing function of α. For more on this point, see the following Chapter.

Let us recall that if $X \sim G(\alpha, \beta)$, then

$$\mathbf{E}[X] = \frac{\beta}{\alpha}, \qquad \mathbf{V}ar[X] = \frac{\beta}{\alpha^2}.$$

The reproductive property is also useful: if $X_i \sim G(\alpha, \beta_i)$, $i = 1, 2, \ldots, n$, and are independent, then

$$\sum_{i=1}^{n} X_i \sim G(\alpha, \beta),$$

where

$$\beta = \sum_{i=1}^{n} \beta_i.$$

Given that each level behaves as a polyarchy and that there is independence among the members, if ν_1 denotes the numbers of evaluations a project must pass at the first level, then we can write

$$T_1 \| (\nu_1 = h) \sim G(\alpha, h). \qquad (2),$$

where "$\|$" denotes conditioning. The distribution of ν_1 is

$$\mathbf{Pr}[\nu_1 = h] = \begin{cases} pq^{h-1}, & \text{if } 1 \leq h \leq n_1 - 1 \\ q^{n_1 - 1}, & \text{if } h = n_1. \end{cases}$$

It follows that

$$\mathbf{E}[\nu_1] = \frac{1 - q^{n_1}}{1 - q},$$

$$\mathbf{E}[\nu_1^2] = \sum_{i=0}^{n_1 - 1} (2i + 1) q^i$$

$$= \frac{1 + q - q^{n_1}(1 + 2n_1) - q^{n_1 + 1}(1 - 2n_1)}{(1 - q)^2}.$$

Writing (2) in the form
$$T_1\|\nu_1 \sim G(\alpha, \nu_1), \qquad (3)$$

we have
$$\mathbf{E}[T_1\|\nu_1] = \frac{\nu_1}{\alpha},$$

and then
$$\mathbf{E}[T_1] = \frac{1}{\alpha}\mathbf{E}[\nu_1] = \frac{1}{\alpha} \cdot \frac{1-q^{n_1}}{1-q}.$$

Furthermore
$$\mathbf{V}ar[T_1] = \mathbf{V}ar[\mathbf{E}[T_1\|N\nu_1]] + \mathbf{E}[\mathbf{V}ar[T_1\|\nu_1]]$$
$$= \mathbf{V}ar\left[\frac{\nu_1}{\alpha}\right] + \mathbf{E}\left[\frac{\nu_1}{\alpha^2}\right]$$
$$= \frac{1}{\alpha^2}\left[\mathbf{V}ar[\nu_1] + \mathbf{E}[\nu_1]\right].$$

Using (3) we have
$$\frac{T_1}{\nu_1}\bigg\|\nu_1 \sim G(\alpha\nu_1, \nu_1), \qquad (4).$$

$\frac{T_1}{\nu_1}$ is the individual average time spent to evaluate a project. Consequently
$$\mathbf{E}\left[\frac{T_1}{\nu_1}\right] = \frac{1}{\alpha}, \qquad (5)$$

$$\mathbf{V}ar\left[\frac{T_1}{\nu_1}\right] = \mathbf{E}\left[\mathbf{V}ar\left[\frac{T_1}{\nu_1}\bigg\|\nu_1\right]\right] + \mathbf{V}ar\left[\mathbf{E}\left[\frac{T_1}{\nu_1}\bigg\|\nu_1\right]\right] \qquad (6)$$
$$= \mathbf{E}\left[\frac{\nu_1}{\alpha^2\nu_1^2}\right] + \mathbf{V}ar\left[\frac{1}{\alpha}\right]$$
$$= \frac{1}{\alpha^2}\mathbf{E}\left[\frac{1}{\nu_1}\right].$$

Let us note that
$$\mathbf{E}\left[\frac{1}{\nu_1}\right] = 1 - \sum_{i=1}^{n_1-1}\frac{q^i}{i(i+1)}.$$

Now let τ_2 be the individual time in evaluating a project for a member belonging to the second level. We introduce dependence among members of the first and of the second level in the following way

$$\tau_2 \| T_1 \sim G\left(\frac{\nu_1}{T_1}, 1\right). \qquad (7)$$

That is, the individual time in evaluating a project for a member of the second level depends on the individual average time spent at the first level. Then, using (5) and (6), we have

$$\mathbf{E}[\tau_2] = \mathbf{E}\left[\frac{T_1}{\nu_1}\right] = \frac{1}{\alpha} = \mathbf{E}[\tau_1], \qquad (8)$$

$$\mathbf{Var}[\tau_2] = \mathbf{Var}\left[\frac{T_1}{\nu_1}\right] + \mathbf{E}\left[\frac{T_1^2}{\nu_1^2}\right].$$

Since

$$\mathbf{E}\left[\frac{T_1^2}{\nu_1^2}\right] = \mathbf{Var}\left[\frac{T_1}{\nu_1}\right] + \frac{1}{\alpha^2},$$

the result is

$$\mathbf{Var}[\tau_2] = \frac{2}{\alpha^2}\mathbf{E}\left[\frac{1}{\nu_1}\right] + \frac{1}{\alpha^2}. \qquad (9)$$

And so

$$\mathbf{Var}[\tau_2] - \mathbf{Var}[\tau_1] = \frac{2}{\alpha^2}\mathbf{E}\left[\frac{1}{\nu_1}\right] > 0.$$

Now we are interested in evaluating the covariance between τ_2 and T_1, that is, between the individual time in evaluating for a member of the second level and the total time spent at the first level. Let us note that

$$\begin{aligned}
\mathbf{E}[\tau_2 T_1] &= \mathbf{E}[\mathbf{E}[\tau_2 T_1 \| T_1]] \\
&= \mathbf{E}[T_1 \mathbf{E}[\tau_2 \| T_1]] \\
&= \mathbf{E}\left[\frac{T_1^2}{\nu_1}\right] \\
&= \mathbf{E}\left[\mathbf{E}\left[\frac{T_1^2}{\nu_1} \bigg\| \nu_1\right]\right] \\
&= \mathbf{E}\left[\frac{1}{\nu_1}\mathbf{E}[T_1^2 \| \nu_1]\right].
\end{aligned}$$

Now
$$\mathbf{E}[T_1^2\|\nu_1] = \mathbf{V}ar[T_1\|\nu_1] + [\mathbf{E}[T_1\|\nu_1]]^2$$
$$= \frac{\nu_1}{\alpha^2} + \frac{\nu_1^2}{\alpha^2}.$$

Then
$$\mathbf{E}[\tau_2 T_1] = \mathbf{E}\left[\frac{1}{\alpha^2} + \frac{\nu_1}{\alpha^2}\right]$$
$$= \frac{1}{\alpha^2} + \frac{1}{\alpha^2}\mathbf{E}[\nu_1].$$

Consequently
$$\mathbf{Cov}[\tau_2, T_1] = \frac{1}{\alpha^2} > 0.$$

To obtain an index of dependence between the levels it is better to resort to the correlation coefficient ρ between τ_2 and $\frac{T_1}{\nu_1}$. First of all let us note that

$$\mathbf{E}\left[\tau_2 \frac{T_1}{\nu_1}\right] = \mathbf{E}\left[\mathbf{E}\left[\tau_2 \frac{T_1}{\nu_1} \middle\| \nu_1\right]\right]$$
$$= \mathbf{E}\left[\frac{1}{\nu_1}\mathbf{E}[\tau_2 T_1\|\nu_1]\right].$$

Using (3) and a property of conditional expectation (see, *e.g.*, Loève (1978, p. 17)) we can write

$$\mathbf{E}[\tau_2 T_1\|\nu_1] = \mathbf{E}[\mathbf{E}[\tau_2 T_1\|T_1]\|\nu_1]$$
$$= \mathbf{E}[T_1\mathbf{E}[\tau_2\|T_1]\|\nu_1]$$
$$= \mathbf{E}\left[\frac{T_1^2}{\nu_1}\middle\|\nu_1\right]$$
$$= \frac{1}{\nu_1}\mathbf{E}[T_1^2\|\nu_1]$$
$$= \frac{1}{\alpha^2}[1 + \nu_1].$$

Consequently
$$\mathbf{E}\left[\tau_2\frac{T_1}{\nu_1}\right] = \frac{1}{\alpha^2}\left[1 + \mathbf{E}\left[\frac{1}{\nu_1}\right]\right],$$

and
$$\text{Cov}\left[\tau_2, \frac{T_1}{\nu_1}\right] = \frac{1}{\alpha^2}\mathbf{E}\left[\frac{1}{\nu_1}\right] > 0.$$

As a result
$$\rho^2 = \frac{\mathbf{E}\left[\frac{1}{\nu_1}\right]}{1 + 2\mathbf{E}\left[\frac{1}{\nu_1}\right]}.$$

It follows that
$$0 \leq \rho \leq \frac{1}{\sqrt{3}}.$$

Furthermore, using the results given in Appendix 1 and 2 it is seen that ρ is an increasing function of p and a decreasing function of n_1.

3. Making the skills variable

For the sake of simplicity we consider a pyramid with just two levels. Now we introduce a dependence among the two levels assuming that the probability of making the wrong decision for the members of the second level depends on the number of evaluations the project had to pass at the first level. If the first level is composed of n members, then
$$\tilde{q} = q^{n-\nu_1}.$$

That means that
$$\tilde{q} = \begin{cases} 1, & \text{if } \nu_1 = n \\ q, & \text{if } \nu_1 = n-1 \\ < q, & \text{otherwise.} \end{cases}$$

Clearly
$$\tilde{q} \geq q \quad \text{if} \quad n = 2.$$

The meaning of this assumption is the following: if $n > 2$, the number of evaluations a project has to pass at the first level is interpreted as an indication of the badness of the project. Therefore, unless the skills of the members of the first level are very low, there is a tendency towards increasing probability to make the right decision for the members of the second level.

It follows, using Appendix 4,

$$\mathbf{E}[\tilde{q}] = q^n \mathbf{E}[q^{-\nu_1}] = q^n \left(n\frac{p}{q} + 1 \right).$$

In Appendix 5 it is proved that this expected value is an increasing function of q and a decreasing function of n.

If the number of members of the second level is m, denoting with ν_2 the number of evaluations of the second level, we have

$$\mathbf{E}[\nu_2 \| \tilde{q}] = 1 + \tilde{q} + \tilde{q}^2 + \ldots + \tilde{q}^{m-1}.$$

Consequently

$$\mathbf{E}[\nu_2] = 1 + \sum_{k=1}^{m-1} q^{kn} \mathbf{E}[q^{-k\nu_1}],$$

where

$$\mathbf{E}[q^{-k\nu_1}] = \left(\frac{1}{q^k} - 1\right) \frac{1 - \left(\frac{1}{q^{k-1}}\right)^n}{1 - \frac{1}{q^{k-1}}} + 1.$$

Refer to Appendix 4.

4. Making the composition of each level variable

Now let the number of members of the second level be a random variable, to be denoted by $\mathcal{M}_2$. Let us set

$$\mathcal{M}_2 = \nu_1,$$

so that

$$\mathcal{M}_2 \leq n.$$

It follows

$$\mathbf{E}[\mathcal{M}_2] = \frac{1 - q^n}{1 - q}.$$

Furthermore

$$\nu_2 \| \mathcal{M}_2 \sim \nu(p, \mathcal{M}_2).$$

It follows that (see Appendix 3)

$$\nu_2 \sim \nu(1 - q^2, n).$$

Then
$$\mathbf{E}[\nu_2] = \frac{1-q^{2n}}{1-q^2} < \mathbf{E}[\nu_1] = \frac{1-q^n}{1-q}.$$

This last result is due to the fact that $\mathbf{E}[\nu_1]$ is an increasing function of q; since $\mathbf{E}[\nu_2]$ is obtained substituting q with q^2 we get the above inequality.

Now let us consider a pyramid with 3 levels. Let $\mathcal{M}_3$ be the number of members of the third level. We define
$$\mathcal{M}_3 = \min(\nu_1, \nu_2) = \nu_2,$$
since
$$\nu_2 \leq \nu_1.$$
Then
$$\mathcal{M}_3 \leq \mathcal{M}_2 \leq n.$$
Consequently
$$\mathbf{E}[\mathcal{M}_3] = \frac{1-q^{2n}}{1-q^2}.$$
Furthermore
$$\nu_3 \| \mathcal{M}_3 \sim \nu(p, \mathcal{M}_3),$$
and, using again Appendix 3,
$$\nu_3 \sim \nu(1-q^3, n).$$
It follows
$$\mathbf{E}[\nu_3] = \frac{1-q^{3n}}{1-q^3}.$$

We can generalize for a pyramid with k levels in the following way. Let us define the number of members $\mathcal{M}_{h+1}$ of the arbitrary level $h+1$ as
$$\mathcal{M}_{h+1} = \min_{1 \leq i \leq h}(\nu_i).$$
Then
$$\mathcal{M}_{h+1} = \nu_h,$$
and
$$n \geq \mathcal{M}_2 \geq \ldots \mathcal{M}_h \geq \mathcal{M}_{h+1}.$$

It follows that
$$\nu_h \sim \nu(1-q^h, n),$$
and so
$$\mathbf{E}[\mathcal{M}_{h+1}] = \frac{1-q^{hn}}{1-q^h}.$$

Let us assume that the project is good. Let us denote with $\mathcal{P}_{h+1}$ the probability that level $h+1$ accepts the project. Then, using Appendix 4,
$$\begin{aligned}\mathcal{P}_{h+1} &= 1 - \mathbf{E}[q^{\mathcal{M}_{h+1}}] \\ &= 1 - \mathbf{E}[q^{\nu_h}] \\ &= \frac{(1-q)(1-q^{n(h+1)})}{1-q^{h+1}}.\end{aligned}$$

Now let $\mathcal{P}$ denote the probability that the pyramid as a whole accepts the project. Since the levels act among themselves as a hierarchy, we have
$$\mathcal{P} = (1-q^n) \prod_{i=1}^{k} \frac{(1-q)(1-q^{ni})}{1-q^i}.$$

5. An application

As an application of the previous results, let us consider a pyramid with $k=2$ levels, following the mechanism described in Section 4. Again, let the project under scrutiny be good and assume that in case of rejection there follows a cost $\gamma > 0$. For simplicity, we assume that the payoff in case of a right decision is equal to zero. Along with this cost, there is another one represented by the wages payed to the members of the pyramid. Since the number of members is now a random variable, the total amount of wages is too. Let $\mathcal{P}$ be the probability that the pyramid accepts the project, thus the expected cost associated to the goodness of the decision is
$$\begin{aligned}\mathbf{E}[C] &= \gamma(1-\mathcal{P}) \\ &= \gamma - \gamma(1-q^n)\frac{1-q^{2n}}{1+q}.\end{aligned}$$

Let $\mathcal{N}$ be the total number of members. Then in expected terms

$$\mathbf{E}[\mathcal{N}] = n + \frac{1-q^n}{1-q}.$$

If we set the individual salary equal to one, then the expected total cost associated to the decision process is given by

$$\mathbf{E}[TC] = \gamma - \gamma(1-q^n)\frac{1-q^{2n}}{1+q} + n + \frac{1-q^n}{1-q}.$$

We can assume that the number of members of the first level n is the parameter under control of the entrepreneur. So it is interesting to study the behavior of $\mathbf{E}[TC]$ for variations in n. We are looking for the optimal n, that is the value which minimizes the expected total cost. It turns out, as expected, that this optimal n depends both on γ and $q = 1-p$. Roughly speaking, the optimal n increases as γ and q increase, as is shown in the following Fig. 1.

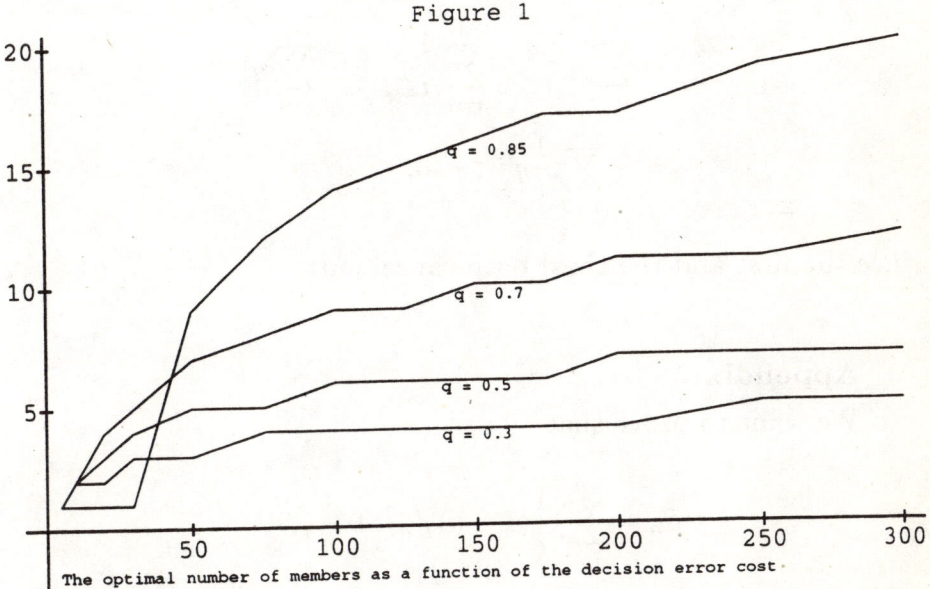

Figure 1

The optimal number of members as a function of the decision error cost

Appendix 1

We want to prove that

$$S = \sum_{i=1}^{n-1} \frac{1}{i} p q^{i-1} + \frac{1}{n} q^{n-1}$$

is a decreasing function of q. We can write S in the following form

$$S = \sum_{i=1}^{n-1} \frac{1}{i}(1-q) q^{i-1} + \frac{1}{n} q^{n-1}$$

$$= \sum_{i=1}^{n} \frac{1}{i} q^{i-1} - \sum_{i=1}^{n-1} \frac{1}{i} q^{i}.$$

Taking the derivative with respect to q we get

$$\frac{\partial S}{\partial q} = \sum_{i=2}^{n} \frac{i-1}{i} q^{i-2} - \sum_{i=1}^{n-1} q^{i-1}$$

$$= \sum_{i=2}^{n} q^{i-2} - \sum_{i=2}^{n} \frac{1}{i} q^{i-2} - \sum_{i=1}^{n-1} q^{i-1}$$

$$= -\sum_{i=2}^{n} \frac{1}{i} q^{i-2} < 0,$$

since the first and the third term cancel out.

Appendix 2

We want to prove that

$$S_n = \sum_{i=1}^{n} \frac{1}{i}(1-q) q^{i-1} + \frac{1}{n} q^{n-1}$$

decreases as n increases. To do that it is enough to prove that $\forall\ n$

$$S_n > S_{n+1}.$$

Clearly

$$S_n - S_{n+1} = -\frac{1}{n}(1-q)q^{n-1} + \frac{1}{n}q^{n-1} - \frac{1}{n+1}q^n$$
$$= q^n\left(\frac{1}{n} - \frac{1}{n+1}\right) > 0,$$

and this proves our assertion.

Appendix 3

Let $\nu(p, n)$ denote the number of evaluations in a polyarchy with n members and p the individual probability to make the right decision. Let

$$\nu_1 \sim \nu(p, n).$$

If

$$\nu_2 \| \nu_1 \sim \nu(p, \nu_1),$$

then

$$\nu_2 \sim \nu(1-q^2, n).$$

Proof

The distribution of ν_1 is

$$\mathbf{Pr}[\nu_1 = k] = \begin{cases} pq^{k-1}, & \text{if } k \leq n-1 \\ q^{n-1}, & \text{if } k = n. \end{cases}$$

The joint distribution of ν_1 and ν_2 is

$$\mathbf{Pr}[\nu_1 = k \cap \nu_2 = i] = \begin{cases} p^2 q^{k-1} q^{i-1}, & \text{if } i < k < n \\ pq^{i-1}q^{n-1}, & \text{if } i < k = n \\ pq^{2(i-1)}, & \text{if } i = k < n \\ q^{2(n-1)}, & \text{if } i = k = n \\ 0, & \text{otherwise.} \end{cases}$$

Then

$$\mathbf{Pr}[\nu_2 = i < n] = pq^{i-1}q^{n-1} + pq^{2(i-1)} + p^2 q^{i-1}\sum_{k=i+1}^{n-1} q^{k-1}$$
$$= (1-q^2)q^{2(i-1)},$$
$$\mathbf{Pr}[\nu_2 = n] = q^{2(n-1)},$$

and this proves our assertion.

Appendix 4

The moment generating function of $\nu(p, n)$ as defined before is

$$G_\nu(t) = \mathbf{E}[e^{t\nu}]$$
$$= (e^t - 1)\frac{1 - (qe^t)^n}{1 - qe^t} + 1.$$

Let us note that

$$\lim_{t \to -\log q} G_\nu(t) = n\frac{p}{q} + 1,$$

that is

$$\mathbf{E}[q^{-\nu}] = n\frac{p}{q} + 1.$$

Furthermore

$$\mathbf{E}[q^{-2\nu}] = \frac{1}{q^{n+1}} + \frac{1}{q^n} - \frac{1}{q},$$

and generally

$$\mathbf{E}[a^\nu] = G_\nu(\log a).$$

Appendix 5

We have

$$\frac{\partial \mathbf{E}[\tilde{q}]}{\partial n} = q^n \frac{1-q}{q} + q^n \left(1 + \frac{n(1-q)}{q}\right) \log q$$
$$= \frac{q^n}{1-p}[p + (1 - p + np)\log(1 - p)].$$

Since $\log(1 - p) < 0$, it is easily seen that the part in brackets attains it maximum when $n = 1$. For this n its value is

$$p + \log(1 - p).$$

Using the series

$$\log(1 - p) = -\left[p + \frac{p^2}{2} + \frac{p^3}{3} + \ldots\right],$$

we see that the quantity in brackets is always negative. Thus the expected value of $\tilde{q}$ is a decreasing function of n.

Now

$$\begin{aligned}\frac{\partial \mathbf{E}[\tilde{q}]}{\partial q} &= \frac{nq^n}{q}\left(1+\frac{n(1-q)}{q}\right) - \left(\frac{n(1-q)}{q^2}+\frac{n}{q}\right)q^n \\ &= \frac{nq^n}{q}\frac{1-q}{q}(n-1) > 0,\end{aligned}$$

showing that the expected value is an increasing function of q.

CHAPTER IV

ORGANIZATION, LOYALTY AND EFFICIENCY

1. Introduction

The problem of the coordination of the choices and behavior of different economic agents is one of the most crucial in economic analysis. This problem arises both within the market and within organizations. Within the market, price coordinates the free choices of the agents. The variation of the price permits the consistency of the independent choices of the economic agents. In particular, following Hayek (1945), the price vector represents the information tool which allows the market to reach equilibrium. Therefore, information is a product of the market rather than a premise of the exchange. On the contrary, according to Stiglitz (1987), the price mechanism does not necessarily bring the economic system towards equilibrium when the quality of the product rests on price. An analogous need for coordination also arises within bureaucratic organizations born to overcome the shortcomings of the market.

Following the "new institutional economics" approach, the organization arises as an instrument to reduce the excess of the transaction costs and to control individual opportunism present within the market due to asymmetric information and uncertainty (Coase, 1937; Williamson, 1975, 1985). According to other scholars the firm (and therefore the organization) arises as a tool to fight the moral hazard caused by asymmetric information or by incomplete information (Alchian and Demsetz, 1972; Ross, 1973; Stiglitz, 1974). Still other scholars (Fama and Jensen, 1983; Alchian and Woodward, 1988), maintain that the firm is a "contract nexus" where the employer-employee relation can be explained by the agency theory. This enables the demarcation of contracts between principal and agent in order to curb the opportunism capacity of the agent (Holmstrom, 1979, 1982; Rees, 1985; Shavell, 1979). Traditionally inside the organization, the command mechanism allows coordination of the actions of its employees. Authority is exerted through hierarchy and the use of norms and rules (Mènard, 1994). The labour contract within the organization is an example of an incomplete contract due to asymmetric information, control costs and uncertainty conditions characterising the principal-agent relation. The hierarchical structure is the mechanism which coordinates the employees, but the structure itself is not sufficient to fight the shirking of the agents. To pursue this aim the principal can resort to award and penalty systems that stimulate the agent to identify himself with the organization through loyal behavior, resulting also in the pursuit of the goal of the organization (Simon, 1991). In such cases in the utility function of the agent, together with individual factors, there is also the goal vector of the organization.

In this section we would like to make particular reference to two instruments proposed by economic analysis which may reduce individual shirking: the *efficiency wage* approach and the *share economy* mechanism. Following the efficiency wage approach (Shapiro and Stiglitz, 1984; Yellen, 1984; Calvo, 1985), the principal (the employer) pays the agent (the employee) a wage greater than the Walrasian level so as to stimulate individual effort and to increase the opportunity cost of the fired agent. The principal sustains a greater cost in order to offer more stimulus to the agent. The higher is the efficiency wage the higher is the opportunity cost of the agent if fired, and thus the higher is the incentive to greater effort. According to the share economy approach (Weitzman, 1984) the employee's wage is related to some indicators of the firm profitability: as the profit increases, for example, the monetary wage of the employee increases too. Except for the exogenous elements negatively influencing firm profitability (management defaults, negative market trend) when the employee's effort is greatest, the agent is stimulated to reduce his own shirking. This chapter aims to analyse the role of another tool that can contribute to reducing the employee's shirking: promotion, that is the possibility for an employee to be advanced to a higher level inside the hierarchy. We think that this tool has, from the employee's point of view, some advantages with respect to the above mentioned instruments. Promotion, besides offering an increased monetary wage, actually entails a more prestigious hierarchical and positional status. Promotion implies both an increased monetary income and an increased psychic income. Therefore promotion can contribute to an increase in the identification and the loyalty of the employee more than the efficiency wage mechanism. Furthermore, promotion can be preferable to the share economy policy as it reduces monetary risk for the employee.

This chapter aims to analyse the role of the promotion within a hierarchical structure whose goal is to make decisions, that is to choose among two alternatives. In particular, in such a case the principal pursues two goals: maximizing the quality of the choice (reducing the probability of making the wrong decision), and choosing correctly and quickly. The quality of the choice depends on the skill level of the agents, while the quickness of the decision rests on the effort of the agent. We assume that the agent's individual effort depends on the promotion possibilities inside the hierarchical structure. The higher these possibilities the higher the agent's effort and the more intense is his identification with the organization's goals. We consider the effort level as a measure of loyalty. If the agent perceives a fading of these possibilities he keeps on using his skill to the best, but his decision will take more time. Measuring the efficiency of the organization as the sum of two factors, the choice's error average cost and the decision delay cost, it follows that the efficiency of the organization is reduced. Inside a hierarchical structure it is not sufficient to choose correctly. The choice must also be timely. A correct but delayed choice can actually compromise the organization's goals. If the agent faces lesser possibilities of promotion he can substantially follow two behaviors that Hirschman (1970) calls *voice and exit*. The voice is represented by the choice of the agent to delay the decision as an instrument of complaint and pressure, while exit entails that the agent chooses to leave the organization to possibly join another. In this situation the agent faces a twofold trade-off: the delay in the decision (the voice) can entail the dismissal risk (so he has an opportunity cost); exit is possible only if the agent has employment alternatives. The agent's choice is a risky one and requires an appropriate cost-benefit assessment. In this chapter we do not deal with such a problem. Instead we aim to underline the role and the importance of the hierarchical promotion in increasing the efficiency of the organization. In our model the principal has to offer a hierarchical structure which increases the career possibilities perceived by the employees as appropriate and credible, in particular by the employees belonging to the bottom levels of the hierarchy. The originality of the model rests on, beside the use of a probabilistic approach to the problem, the specific measure of efficiency with which to compare different hierarchical structures. Another point we do not examine in this chapter but which is stressed by Radner (1992) is that if the promotion increases the number of hierarchical piers and decisors, it can contribute to a delay in the time of decision making and so reduces efficiency. Radner shows that a decision structure is efficient when, given the number of projects to assess, it is not possible to reduce the number of decisors without augmenting the delay of the decision or viceversa. So the promotion mechanism on the one hand can improve efficiency, and on the other hand can become a further element of cost. But this problem is material for new research. We do not deal with such a trade-off.

The chapter is organised as follows. Section 2 presents the framework of the model. Section 3 introduces the pyramid decision structures. Section 4 presents the measure of loyalty associated to each pyramid structure. Section 5 models the time required to reach a decision. Section 6 defines the expected total cost of the decision and compares the efficiency of different pyramid structures. Section 7 presents final remarks. The Appendices give the formal proofs of the results.

2. The framework of the model

The aim of this chapter is to study the efficiency of hierarchical organizations whose duty it is to make decisions. For our purposes the two variables characterizing efficiency are the individuals' skills and the loyalty of the members of the decision structure. Schematically, the skills are measured by the individual probability to make the right decision (Sah and Siglitz 1985, 1986, 1988a, 1988b), and Sah 1991). Loyalty is measured by the amount of individual effort. At least in the short run skills can be assumed as given, while loyalty may change. So in order to increase efficiency, it is necessary to augment loyalty. The issue of loyalty is related to the goal of each organization to tackle the shirking and moral hazard of the individuals belonging to it. As the economic literature points out (Arrow, 1985; Pauly, 1968), shirking and moral hazard are due to the existence of asymmetric information and the cost of control of the individual behaviour within hierarchical organizations. The entrepreneur can contrast shirking and moral hazard through surveillance (which implies a cost we do not consider in our model), incentives and penalties. Let us note that more generally the loyalty problem is analyzed within the framework of the principal-agent theory (Ross, 1973; Rees, 1985a, 1985b; Levinthal, 1988) and of the labor market theory in relation to wage determination (in particular see the literature on wage efficiency: Shapiro and Stiglitz, 1984; Yellen, 1984; Calvo, 1985; Bowles, 1985; and the literature on the share economy: Weitzman, 1984).

In this chapter no individual can modify his skills, but he can reduce or increase his effort. Increasing effort implies reducing the time required to perform his duty, and viceversa. In our paper, the career perspectives (as perceived by each individual) offered by the organization to its members represent the variable that influences loyalty. A general reference on the changes of loyalty is the paper by Akerlof (1983).

As a result of our assumptions we can measure efficiency in terms of the sum of two expected costs: the expected cost related to the correctness of the decision, and that related to the time required to reach the decision.

The decision structures we are going to analyse are of the pyramid type. As will be described in the following section, our model allows us to compare the efficiency of different pyramid structures.

3. Pyramid decision structures

It is common sense to envisage hierarchy as a pyramid. The top managers examine a project only if all the precedent tiers have approved it. Within each tier the decision process can follow different majority rules. In this paper we chose to assume that each level behaves as a polyarchy. To be more precise, the structure is composed of a series of levels each of which is composed of a number of elements not greater than that of the level immediately below. Now let the decision to be made to be of a dichotomous type, for example to accept or to reject a project. Then each level behaves as a polyarchy, that is the level accepts the project if at least one of its members accepts it. Furthermore the levels act among themselves as a hierarchy, that is the whole structure accepts the project if all the levels accept it. As a matter of convention, let the *bottom level* (or first) be that with the greatest number of elements and the *top level* (or last) that with the lowest number. Given N, the total number of components of the structure, and k, the number of levels, we have different possible configurations of the pyramid, depending on the distribution of the members across the levels. We introduce a *quasi-lexicographic* ordering of configurations which can be identified with a sort of a law of evolution from an originary configuration. The *originary* configuration is characterised as containing just one element at each level, with the exception of the bottom. Thus, this law of evolution can be stated in the following way: from each configuration the next one is obtained through a movement of one unit from the bottom level to that immediately above, if it is possible to maintain a pyramid configuration. If it is not, through a movement of one unit from the second level to the third one, if it is possible ... and so on. We start from the originary configuration and when we reach a configuration that does not allow further movement we say that we have reached a *stable* configuration. In this quasi-lexicographic ordering each configuration is situated in a "dictionary" where the first *word* is the originary configuration and the last word is the stable configuration. To make things clearer we formalize in this way. A *configuration* of the pyramid, given N and k, to be indicated with $\omega(N,k)$, is a set of k numbers: $\{n_1, n_2, \ldots, n_k\}$, such that

$$\sum_{i=1}^{k} n_i = N, \qquad n_1 \geq n_2 \geq \ldots \geq n_k.$$

That is to say, the first number of the set is the number of elements at the bottom level while the last one is that of the elements of the top level, and generally the i-th number is the number of elements of the i-th level, $1 \leq i \leq k$. The originary configuration is

$$\omega_o(N,k) = \{N-k+1, 1, \ldots, 1, 1\}.$$

Hierarchy and polyarchy were introduced by Sah and Stiglitz as particular types of decision structures dealing with dichotomous choices (for example to accept or to reject a project). A polyarchy accepts a project when at least one of its members accepts it while a hierarchy accepts a project when all of its members accept it. For our purposes let us note here that probabilistically a polyarchy is equivalent to a sequence of individual evaluations of a project which stops should a first individual accept the project. On the other hand, a hierarchy is equivalent to a sequence of evaluations that stops when a first individual does not accept the project.

4. A measure of loyalty

Let N and k be given. Let $\{\omega_i(N,k)\}$ be the set of all the configurations that correspond to the steps of our evolution law. In the sequel we drop the arguments N and k. For $i = o$ we have the originary configuration, for $i = s$ we have the stable configuration. An increase of one unit in i corresponds to a step further on in our dictionary.

Now we are going to assign to the set $\{\omega_i\}$ corresponding to a given N and k, a function which is instrumental to the introduction of a measure of loyalty associated to each configuration. Let

$$\omega_i = \{n_{1_i}, n_{2_i}, \ldots, n_{k_i}\}.$$

Then

$$\psi(\omega_i) = \sum_{j=1}^{k}(k+1-j)n_{j_i}. \qquad (1)$$

It is easy to verify, using the sequence which embodies the evolution law described in Appendix 1, that

$$\psi(\omega_{i+1}) = \psi(\omega_i) - 1. \qquad (2)$$

Let us note that

$$\psi(\omega_o) = (N - k + 1)k + \frac{k(k-1)}{2}.$$

The reason why ψ is related to a measure of loyalty associated to each configuration (and loyalty is essentially an increasing function of ψ) is the following.

Loyalty is intrinsically related to the possibility perceived by each member of the structure of advancing to a higher level, that is, to be promoted. This perception is dependent upon the fact that there is room at the levels above. Then it is reasonable to assume that a measure of this possibility is related to the sum of the differences between each level and the top level, plus a measure of the width of the top level. Furthermore, it stands to reason that these differences be weighted differently, in the sense that the perception of a member at the lowest levels is most important. Think for example of the situation in which the lowest level is represented by young people at the beginning of their career. As shown in Appendix 1, these considerations lead to (1).

5. The time necessary to reach a decision

Now we are going to model the total time T spent by configuration ω_i to reach the decision. This total time will be denoted by

$T(\omega_i)$. Let us assume that the time employed by each individual to reach a decision, τ, be distributed as a Gamma variable with parameters α and 1, that is

$$\tau \sim G(\alpha, 1).$$

α is intrinsically related to the loyalty: the greater α the greater the loyalty. Since a greater α implies a higher probability of making the decision in a short period of time, then α depends on the configuration ω_i and it can be written as α_i. We can set

$$\alpha_i = \psi(\omega_i),$$

so that, using (2),

$$\alpha_i > \alpha_{i+1}.$$

This means that loyalty decreases as we move forward in the dictionary of configurations.

The framework to obtain T starting from τ is derived from Sah and Stiglitz. The assumptions are the following. Let the decision to be taken be of a dichotomous type. Let the project under scrutiny be good and let p be the individual probability of accepting a good project (so in this case p is the individual probability of making the right decision). Let the individuals be independent and share the same p.

Given the results in Appendix 2, we can evaluate $\mathbf{E}[T(\omega_i)]$ for each i, that is the expected total time.

6. The total cost

In our pyramids the probability to accept the project, under the assumption that it is good, is given by

$$\prod_{j=1}^{k}(1 - q^{n_j}). \qquad (6)$$

Writing

$$\mathcal{P}(\omega_i) = \prod_{j=1}^{k}(1 - q^{n_{j_i}}),$$

it can be proved that

$$\mathcal{P}(\omega_{i+1}) > \mathcal{P}(\omega_i), \tag{7}$$

with equality only for $p = 1$ or $p = 0$. Now let us write $\mathcal{R}(\omega_i)$ for the probability to reject the project, which is related to a cost for the decision structure. Then

$$\mathcal{R}(\omega_i) = 1 - \mathcal{P}(\omega_i),$$

$$\mathcal{R}(\omega_i) > \mathcal{R}(\omega_{i+1}). \tag{8}$$

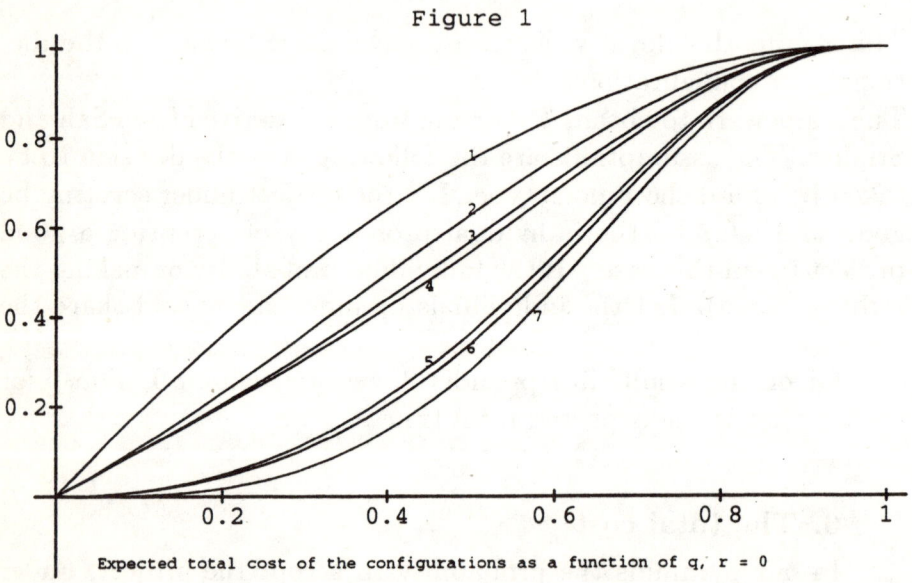

Figure 1

Expected total cost of the configurations as a function of q, r = 0

Let us assume that the right decision does not entail a positive payoff, while there is a negative payoff (a cost) in the case of a wrong decision. Furthermore, let us define this negative payoff as 1. The time spent in reaching a decision is another cost that enters the total cost associated with a decision process. In our model it turns out that the total cost, in expected terms, associated to configuration ω_i is

$$\mathcal{C}(\omega_i) = \mathcal{R}(\omega_i) + r\mathbf{E}[T(\omega_i)], \tag{9}$$

where r is a parameter that weighs the influence of loyalty. Since we set the negative payoff equal to 1, r is essentially the ratio between the cost of the time required to reach a decision (which depends on the loyalty) and the cost of the decision error.

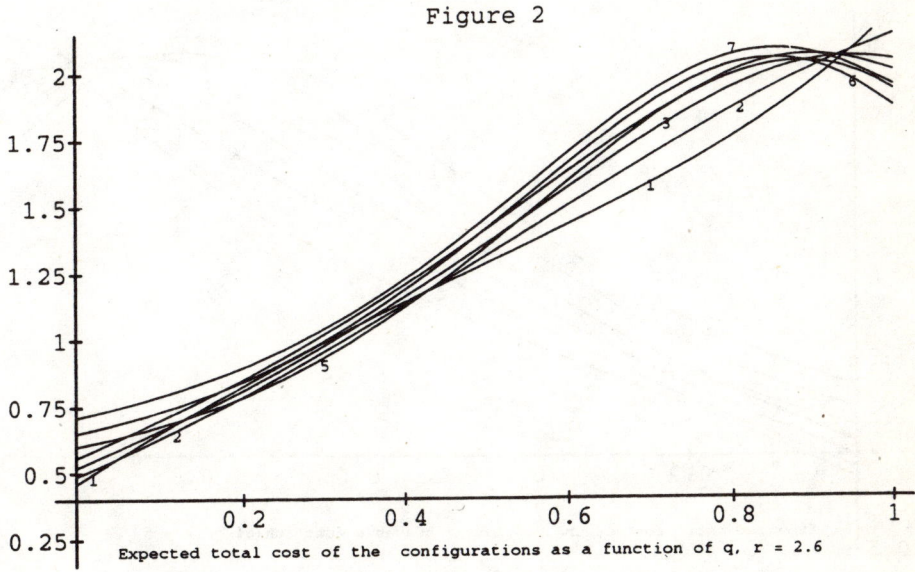

Figure 2

Expected total cost of the configurations as a function of q, r = 2.6

If $r = 0$, using (7) it is easy to see that the most efficient configuration is the stable configuration, whatever the value of p. As r increases, the most preferable configuration depends on the value of p. It is impossible to obtain straightforward results. However, because loyalty decreases as we move forward in the dictionary, we can expect that as r increases the most preferable configurations will be found more and more among the configurations located at the beginning of the dictionary. Numerical analyses in the case $N = 10$ and $k = 3$ show that this is indeed the case. We present a sample of graphs (Figures 1, 2 and 3) corresponding to $r = 0$,

$r = 2.6$ and $r = 5$. Each graph represents the expected total cost as a function of $q = 1 - p$, appearing on the abscissas, for the different configurations (which are 7 when $N = 10$ and $k = 3$). The numbers on the curves identify the configurations. When $r = 5$ we can see that the originary configuration performs better for almost every q value, except for values close to 1. Let us note that with this value of r, and *a fortiori* with greater values, the effect of $\mathcal{R}$ on $\mathcal{C}$ tends to disappear. That means that further increments of r cause only a shift of all the curves.

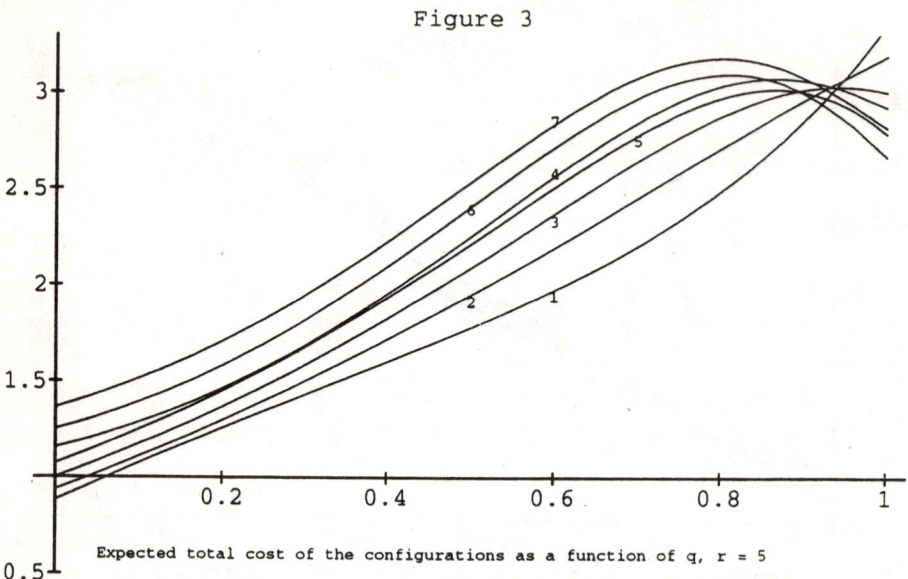

Figure 3

Expected total cost of the configurations as a function of q, r = 5

7. Final remarks

In order to assess the efficiency of hierarchical organizations whose duty it is to make decisions, we specified two variables: the correctness of the decision made and the loyalty of the members. Essentially, correctness is defined probabilistically as the probability of making the right decision; in this way it depends on the individual skills, measured by the individual probability p, which is given, of making the right decision. We assume that each member of the organization always acts to the best of his abilities, while the intensity of his efforts is variable. In our model loyalty is represented by this intensity. We built a model which takes into account how different structures of organizations influence these two variables. More precisely, we characterised the organizations as pyramid structures, that is a series of levels whose composition does not increase. The operational feature is that each level behaves as a polyarchy, and the levels among them behave as a hierarchy.

Given N, the total number of members of the organization, and k, the number of levels, we were able to define a quasi-lexicographic ordering of the resulting configurations, that is the different distributions of members across the levels subject to some specified restriction. In this ordering the first configuration has a large base and a very slim top, while the last configuration is more evenly distributed and has a stocky appearance. With the assumption that the project under scrutiny is good we proved that correctness increases moving towards the stocky configuration.

We defined a measure that associates a value of loyalty to each configuration. Such a measure is explained by the fact that each configuration implies different career prospects as perceived by the individuals. The stronger this perception, the higher the loyalty. We show that loyalty decreases moving towards the stocky configuration.

For the sake of convenience, we assumed that the payoff resulting from a right decision is 0, while in the case of a wrong decision the payoff (cost) is 1. Furthermore we defined a cost relative to the time required to make the decision. The sum of these two costs, in expected terms, measures efficiency. More flexibility is obtained by introducing a parameter weighing the influence of loyalty. As a result, we studied and compared the efficiency of the configurations as a function of this parameter.

We can sum up the main results as follows. The stocky configuration is the most efficient when this parameter is 0. As this parameter increases, there is no configuration uniformly superior (with respect to the individual probability p) to the others, but the dominant configurations are to be found among those of the stocky type. Further increases of the parameter cause a progressive shift of dominance towards the slim configurations. For sufficiently large values of the parameter, the first configuration (the slimmest one) appears to be the most efficient for almost all p values, except for values very close to 0.

Appendix 1

The evolution law from the originary configuration, as described, means that we have the sequence

(1) n_1 decreases, n_2 increases, n_3 is constant, ..., n_k is constant,

(2) n_1 is constant, n_2 decreases, n_3 increases, ..., n_k is constant,

(3) n_1 is constant, n_2 is constant, n_3 decreases, ..., n_k is constant,

......

again (1), (2), (3), ..., until reaching the stable configuration.
Remark. The last configuration of each group is the first of the following group.

As we said in Section 4, loyalty is intrinsically related to the perceived possibility to advance to a higher level. This perception hinges upon the fact that there is room on the levels above. Thus it is reasonable to assume that a measure of this possibility is related to the sum of the differences between each level and the top level, plus a measure of the width of the top level. Furthermore, it stands to reason to weight these differences differently, in the sense that the perception of a member who is situated at the lowest levels is most important. These considerations lead us to define the following measure of loyalty associated to the configuration ω_i, $\omega_i = \{n_{1_i}, n_{2_i}, \ldots, n_{k_i}\}$:

$$\sum_{j=1}^{k-1}(k+1-j)(n_{j_i} - n_{k_i}) + cn_{k_i}.$$

This expression reduces to

$$\sum_{j=1}^{k-1}(k+1)n_{j_i} - \sum_{j=1}^{k-1}jn_{j_i} - (k-1)(k+1)n_{k_i} + \frac{k(k-1)}{2}n_{k_i} + cn_{k_i}.$$

Setting
$$c = 1 - \frac{k(k-1)}{2} + (k-1)(k+1)$$
we obtain (1) of Section 4.

Appendix 2

Let us assume that the time employed by an individual to reach a decision, τ, be distributed as a Gamma variable with parameters α and 1, that is
$$\tau \sim G(\alpha, 1).$$
Let us note here the reproductive property of the Gamma distribution, that is, if $X_i \sim G(\alpha, \beta_i)$ and are independent, then
$$\sum_{i=1}^{n} X_i \sim G(\alpha, \beta),$$
where
$$\beta = \sum_{i=1}^{n} \beta_i.$$
Furthermore
$$\mathbf{E}[X_i] = \frac{\beta_i}{\alpha}, \qquad \mathbf{V}ar[X_i] = \frac{\beta_i}{\alpha^2}.$$
Consequently
$$\mathbf{E}[\tau] = \frac{1}{\alpha}, \qquad \mathbf{V}ar[\tau] = \frac{1}{\alpha^2}.$$

Now let the decision to be made be of a dichotomous type. Let the project under scrutiny be good and let p be the individual probability of accepting a good project (so in this case p is the individual probability to make the right decision). Let the individuals be independent and share the same p. Now let the decision structure be a polyarchy with n members. Let ν be the number of evaluations a project has to pass, and furthermore let T_P be the total time employed by the structure to reach a decision. The assumption of independence among the members and what was said at the end of Section 3 imply

$$T_P \| (\nu = h) \sim G(\alpha, h), \qquad 1 \leq h \leq n \tag{1}$$

where "$\|$" means *conditioning*. The distribution of ν is

$$\mathbf{Pr}[\nu = h] = pq^{h-1}, \qquad 1 \leq h \leq n-1$$
$$\mathbf{Pr}[\nu = n] = q^{n-1},$$

where $q = 1 - p$. Writing (1) in the form

$$T_P \| \nu \sim G(\alpha, \nu), \tag{2}$$

we have

$$\mathbf{E}[T_P \| \nu] = \frac{\nu}{\alpha},$$

and then

$$\mathbf{E}[T_P] = \frac{1}{\alpha} \mathbf{E}[\nu] = \frac{1}{\alpha} \cdot \frac{1 - q^n}{1 - q}.$$

Let us note that $\mathbf{E}[\nu]$ increases as q and n increase. Furthermore

$$\mathbf{Var}[T_P] = \mathbf{Var}[\mathbf{E}[T_P \| \nu]] + \mathbf{E}[\mathbf{Var}[T_P \| \nu]]$$
$$= \mathbf{Var}\left[\frac{\nu}{\alpha}\right] + \mathbf{E}\left[\frac{\nu}{\alpha^2}\right]$$
$$= \frac{1}{\alpha^2} \left[\mathbf{Var}[\nu] + \mathbf{E}[\nu]\right].$$

Since

$$\mathbf{E}[T_P \nu] = \mathbf{E}[\nu \mathbf{E}[T_P \| \nu]]$$
$$= \mathbf{E}[\nu \frac{\nu}{\alpha}] = \frac{1}{\alpha} \mathbf{E}[\nu^2],$$

it follows, denoting with ρ the coefficient of correlation between T and ν, that $\rho > 0$, and

$$\rho^2 = \frac{\mathbf{Var}[\nu]}{\mathbf{Var}[\nu] + \mathbf{E}[\nu]}.$$

Let us note that

$$\mathbf{E}[\nu^2] = \sum_{i=0}^{n-1}(2i+1)q^i.$$

Let us now turn to our pyramid structures. Let T_j the total time employed by level j to reach a decision, and let T be the total time employed by the pyramid. We have

$$E[T] = E[T_1] + E[T_2] \cdot \mathbf{Pr}[A_1] + E[T_3] \cdot \mathbf{Pr}[A_1] \cdot \mathbf{Pr}[A_2] + \ldots \quad (3)$$
$$+ E[T_k] \cdot \mathbf{Pr}[A_1] \cdot \mathbf{Pr}[A_2] \cdots \mathbf{Pr}[A_{k-1}],$$

where

$$E[T_j] = \frac{1}{\alpha} \cdot \frac{1-q^{n_j}}{1-q}, \qquad \mathbf{Pr}[A_j] = 1 - q^{n_j}.$$

The α appearing in (3) is related to the loyalty and so it depends on the configuration ω_i, thus it can be written as α_i. We can set

$$\alpha_i = \psi(\omega_i),$$

so that, using (2) of Section 4,

$$\alpha_i > \alpha_{i+1}.$$

If $T(\omega_i)$ denotes the total time employed by configuration ω_i, we can evaluate $\mathbf{E}[T(\omega_i)]$ for each i using (3) with α_i in place of α.

The ordering of $\mathbf{E}[T(\omega_i)]$ depends on p; there are no straightforward results. Let us write ω_1 for ω_o and ω_z for ω_s, where $z = \mu(N, k)$ as defined in Section 4. Numerical analysis shows, assuming $\alpha_i = 1$, $\forall i$, that ω_1 and ω_z are superior to all other configurations, ω_z for low values of p and ω_1 for high values. If we discard these two configurations, then ω_2 and ω_{z-1} are superior to all the others, ω_{z-1} for low values of p and ω_2 for high values, and so on. Since $\alpha_i > \alpha_{i+1}$, it turns out that for high values of p the superior configuration is ω_1. Actually our numerical analysis shows that this is so only for values of p close to zero.

CONCLUSIONS

The quality of human decisions and, consequently, the quality of the decisions made by organizations, rests substantially on the following elements: the presence of uncertainty, the existence of asymmetric information, the skills of the decisors, the time necessary to reach a decision and the level of identification of the decisors with the goal pursued by the organization. In fact, these elements can be considered inputs for the production of the output represented by the decision. The quality of the decision (that is, its correctness) can therefore be improved by increasing the quality of the inputs. For example, the availability of greater and better information contributes, coeteris paribus, to the improved quality of the decision. However, increasing the quality and the quantity of inputs incurs additional costs. Thus, a decisor with better skills has a greater probability to choose correctly, coeteris paribus, but entails a larger salary. Each decision to be made implies a trade-off between the increment of the quality of the inputs and the increased cost incurred to finance the growth of quality. Due to this cost and to the scarcity of available resources, human decisions are necessarily subject to errors.

The quality of decisions made within an organization is influenced by an additional factor: the typology of the organization. In terms of correctness of the decision it is not indifferent to decide through a hierarchy or a polyarchy instead of through a committee or through some mix of these elementary forms. Two other elements influence the quality of decisions made by organizations: the enforced majority rule, and the nature of the relationship among the different members of the organization. More specifically, the majority rule affects the time necessary to reach a decision: it can take more time to reach an unanimous decision than a simple majority. With respect to the relationship among the members of the organization, cooperation among members and their level of effort are likely to increase as their identification with the goal of the organization increases. Consequently, the time required to reach a decision decreases, coeteris paribus. As loyalty of the members grows, so does the quality of the decision.

The likelihood of making the correct decision (in our book we have dealt only with dichotomous choices) depends on which of the three elementary forms of organizations (hierarchy, polyarchy, committee) is at work. In order to compare the three forms it is worthwhile to consider another factor: the quality of the portfolio. The quality of the portfolio is defined as the expected value of the benefit of a project randomly drawn from a portfolio containing a given number of profitable and unprofitable projects. When the expected value is equal to zero, the portfolio's quality is neutral, that is, the positive expected benefit equals the negative expected benefit. When the expected value is greater than zero we can define the quality as good; otherwise, when the expected value is negative, the quality is considered bad.

Using binomial distribution, one easily ranks the three elementary forms in decreasing order of probability of accepting a project (either profitable or unprofitable): polyarchy, committee (with a consensus level strictly greater than one and lesser than n), hierarchy.

Obviously, in the presence of a high quality portfolio it is desirable to have a higher probability of accepting a project. Thus, the higher the portfolio's quality, the higher the performance of a polyarchy relative to that of a committee, and the higher the performance of a committee relative to that of a hierarchy.

Extending our analysis, let us assume that each single evaluation of a project entails a cost. There is a fundamental difference between the performance of a committee as opposed to a polyarchy or hierarchy, with respect to the expected evaluation cost per project. In a committee, evaluations occur simultaneously, while in both a polyarchy and in a hierarchy the evaluations follow specific sequential patterns. As a consequence the committee requires a greater number of evaluations than either a polyarchy or a hierarchy, and the evaluation cost per project is therefore higher.

Another useful element in the assessment of the performance of the three elementary forms is the total time required by each organisation to make a decision. Generally sequential decision structures entail incremental time delay, which can prove significant. The time delay entails an additional cost, proportional to the length of the sequence of assessments through which a project must pass. Thus, the committee presents the smallest time delay cost, while the hierarchy presents the highest time delay cost. Polyarchy is located between these two extremes.

In the second part of the book we present a model by which we analyse the performance of a particular form of decision organization, the pyramid decision structure. This structure combines features of the elementary forms of hierarchy and polyarchy. More precisely, we layered different organizational levels in a pyramid form: each level behaves as a polyarchic structure, while the relationship among the levels is hierarchical. Given the number of organizational levels and the total number of members of the entire organization we built a quasi-lexicographic ordering of the different configurations. We were then able to compare the relative performance of the different configurations in terms of both the accuracy of the decision and of the time required to reach it.

Results.

In Chapter I and Chapter II of Part I we discuss how and when special majority rules are advantageous. Generally, a special majority rule requires more time to reach a decision than a simple majority rule. In Chapter I we model this additional time as the process by which the leader influences the other members' choice. In Chapter II, this additional time is determined by the number of times the decision structure must be reconvened before reaching a decision. We show that in both models the determination of the most advantageous majority rule rests on the ratio between the cost due to the delay and the cost associated with the wrong decision. The advantage of more stringent majority rules increases when this ratio decreases. The simplified model presented in Chapter I of Part I confirms our intuition that decisions over relevant matters require slanted procedures. In particular (except for a restricted range of values of the parameters) the higher the *error cost*, the more likely it is that unanimity is the more advantageous procedural rule. Our model shows that the indifference value of the *error cost* (that is, the value of the error cost such that the procedural rules perform equally well) decreases as the relative leadership (the ratio between the difference of the skills of the different members and of the leader's skills) increases. The intuition underlying the main results of Chapter I is that, given the particular composition of the decision structure (the leadership's characteristics and role), unanimity rule gives power to the most skillful member and therefore increases the probability of making the right decision. When the cost of making the wrong decision is sufficiently high, unanimity is therefore better.

In Chapter II of Part I we analysed how majority rules affect efficiency in the decision process of a decision body (composed by n members with the same goal) facing a dichotomous choice. Our assumptions are as follows. All n members of the decision body have the same probability of making the right decision, and choose independently from each other. We can write the expected total cost of the decision process as the sum of two components: the expected cost related to the correctness of the decision made, and the cost of the expected time necessary to reach the decision. The majority rule that minimizes the expected total cost is defined as advantageous. In Chapter I of Part I we presented another model to study the same problem. The assumptions were as follows. All members but one of the decision body are homogeneous with respect to their skills, and decide independently from each other. The one with greater skills acts as the leader and influences the decision of the other members. In both models the majority rules more stringent than the simple majority entail a cost as an increasing function of the delay in reaching the decision. In Chapter II we model the delay as a random variable which describes the time necessary to reach the required majority. For the model presented in Chapter I, using a stochastic process, we modelled how some members change their initial opinion under the influence of a leader, making it possible to reach the required majority. The behaviour of the members affected by the leader is described by a Markov Chain. To sum up: both models show that the determination of the most advantageous majority rule rests on the ratio between the cost due to the delay and the cost associated with the wrong decision. The advantage of more stringent majority rules increases when this ratio decreases. In the model presented in Chapter I the strength of leadership is a factor which reduces the cost due to delay.

We would like to emphasize that the problem dealt with in our analysis belongs to the economic literature referred to Sah and Stiglitz (1986, 1988a, 1988b) as "the architecture of the economic systems". More particularly, Chapter II is akin to their research in the determination of the optimal consensus level of a committee composed of n members. We share the same initial assumptions, although we do not differentiate between Type I and Type II errors. Instead, we explicitly introduce the cost due to the likely delay incurred when the required majority is more stringent than the simple one.

In Chapter III of Part I we outline the owner's dilemma in comparing the performance of two decision organisations: one composed of members acting independently, the other one made up of members working together cooperatively in presence of a leader. In this model, the additional salary to employ the leader must also be taken into account. Analysis has shown that the trade-off between cooperation and independence is not trivial. Given n (the number of members in the decision structure), the choice of cooperation *versus* independence depends on several variables: k (the consensus level), p (the probability of accepting a good project), π (the proportion of good projects in the portfolio), z (the benefit flow originating from a good project), and w (the additional cost of employing a leader).

If $w = 0$ (no additional cost for the leader) the preference for a particular decision structure depends only on the respective probabilities $\mathcal{P}^T$ and $\mathcal{P}^I$ of accepting a good project (the apices T and I denote a structure characterized by cooperation or independence, respectively). For simplicity let us assume n is odd, and call $(n+1)/2$ the *simple majority rule* (*s.m.r.*). Now

i) if $k < $ s.m.r. then the minimum value of p (p_m) such that $\mathcal{P}^T < \mathcal{P}^I$ is less than $1/2$: $p_m \to 0$ as $k \to 1$;

ii) if $k = $ s.m.r. then $p_m = 1/2$;

iii) if $k > $ s.m.r. then $p_m > 1/2$ and $p_m \to 1$ as $k \to n$ (unanimity).

If $w > 0$, the preference of one decision structure over another also depends on π and z. With the *simple majority rule*, a necessary condition for preferring cooperation over independence is that $p < 1/2$. As w increases, the interval of the values of p such that cooperation is preferred to independence, becomes narrower.

The effect of w on the length of such an interval can be offset by relatively high values of π and z.

Chapter IV of Part I is essentially an extension of Condorcet's jury theorem. The assumption of independence among the members is relaxed, and the members are not required to be homogeneous. The probabilistic tool used in modelling is that of conditional independence. Here, too, we have the presence of a leader. The resulting correlation among the members is studied, and the distribution of the number of votes of the same type is examined. We show that, in the range of values relevant for our parameters, this distribution is bimodal. We are concerned with the type of decision that has to be made by a group of people such as the members of a board or of a committee, or jurors in a criminal trial. The decision is typically of the dichotomic type; such as whether to accept or reject a project, or whether to absolve or convict a defendant. There is a good deal of literature on the different facets of this problem. Here, more than usual, it is important to clarify the assumptions on which we modelled the object under analysis. One assumption concerns the independence of the members, such that there is no influence among them. Another is related to the problem of modelling individual skills. We follow the approach whereby skills may be represented by two numbers, the probabilities of Type I error and of Type II error, or, simply, by one number which reflects the probability of making the correct decision.

Here is a brief listing of some of the main contributions on this topic, which may help to delineate the principal lines of analysis. For independence and homogeneity the problem of structure (polyarchy, hierarchy or committee) is analyzed in Sah and Stiglitz (*e.g.* 1986, 1988*a*, 1988*b*). The same authors discuss the problem of the level of consensus in an analysis of committees. Nitzan and Paroush (1982) define the optimal weighted majority rule, which is a simple majority rule that allows for different weights of members' decisions. In the same context, Karotkin (1993) discusses the inferiority of restricted majority rules (chairman rule, expert rule and others). Regarding dependence and homogeneity, Berg (1993*a*, 1993*b*, 1994) proves an extension of Condorcet's jury theorem. A simpler model of dependence is given by Boland (1989) and Boland et al. (1989) (in a discussion of deference voting).

In Chapter IV we constructed another more detailed model of dependence, which permits a certain amount of dishomogeneity. The probabilistic tool used in modelling is that of conditional independence. In this respect our approach is close to that of Berg (who uses the Polya- Eggenberger's urn model). However, we also consider a very special member, the leader, whose choice influences that of the other members. We studied the resulting correlation among members and how it can be encompassed by a function of the parameters of the model. Finally, we devised a simple scheme by which we could confront the different weighted majority rules.

In Chapter V of Part I we present a model that particularly suits the decision process of political organisations such as parties, whose members share a common ideology. It studies the effect of the introduction of a dependence on the probability of making the right decision, and on the expected number of evaluations a project must pass before a decision is made. This dependence is introduced by means of the Polya-Eggenberger's urn model. A parameter of this model can be assumed as a measure of the dependence. In this chapter we also studied the effect of the introduction of dependence among members of a decision making structure on the probability of making the right decision and on the expected number of evaluations a project must pass before a decision is made. The decision making structures considered are polyarchies, hierarchies and committees (for simplicity, only committees with a consensus level equal to 2). In the case of polyarchies and hierarchies, we get very clear results. In both structures the expected number of evaluations increases as dependence increases. In contrast, in the case of polyarchies, the probability of making the right decision decreases as dependence increases, while the contrary is true for hierarchies. As for committees, the results are less clear. The behavior of the expected number of evaluations, as a function of the parameter measuring dependence, depends on individual precision or skill, which can be measured by the individual probability of making the right decision. We can say that with a high individual precision, this expected number is an increasing function of the dependence; in the case of low individual precision, the opposite is true. Moving from high individual precision to low individual precision the results vary.

In Chapter I and II of Part II we propose a model of pyramidal organisations. In these Chapters we maintain the basic assumptions of Section 2 of the Introduction. Given the total number of members and the number of levels of the pyramid, we consider the different distributions of members across the levels obeying the rule characterising a pyramid. We show that these configurations can be *genetically* ordered, moving from a configuration that can be considered originary up to a configuration that can be considered stable. We then state what can be considered an evolutionary law governing the pyramid. This ordering turns out to be consistent with the probability of accepting a good project and the probability of rejecting a bad project. Even the expected number of evaluations, in some respects, is consistently ordered.

The results obtained can be a good starting point for the modelling of the dynamics of decision structures.

The *evolution law* can be understood to be the result of the interaction between the members' desire for promotion (to move from one level of the configuration to the a higher one), and the economic and strategic calculus of the entrepreneur.

The substance of Chapter III of Part II consists in a continued analysis of pyramidal organisations, relaxing some of the above mentioned basic assumptions. Essentially, we introduce some models of dependence. In the first model, the intensity of each member's effort is made variable, depending on the degree of the loyalty of the members with respect to the entire structure. A second model makes the individual skills variable and, finally, a third model makes the composition of each level variable, within the obvious constraints imposed by the pyramid rule. An application is then offered.

In Chapter IV of Part II we show that it is possible to make each configuration correspond to a degree of loyalty. Loyalty can be understood as follows: the member's individual effort depends on the promotion potential within the pyramidal organisation. The higher is this potential the higher is the member's effort and the more intense is his identification with the organisation's goals. In our model the effort level is a measure of loyalty. Our pyramidal organisations pursue the goal of maximising the efficiency of the decision process. Efficiency is defined as a combination of the correctness of the decision and the velocity of the decision. The aim of Chapter IV is to compare the efficiency level of the different configurations, keeping in mind that a specific degree of loyalty corresponds to each configuration, and hence to a specific degree of velocity.

In order to assess the decision making efficiency of hierarchical organizations, we specify two variables: the correctness of the made decision and the loyalty of the members. Correctness can essentially be defined as the probability of making the right decision. It thus depends on the individual skills, measured by the given individual probability p of making the right decision. We assume that each member of the organization always acts to the best of his abilities while the intensity of his efforts is variable, and in our model this intensity represents the degree of loyalty. We build a model which takes into account the influence of different organisational structures on these two variables. More precisely, we characterise the organizations as pyramid structures, whereby each level behaves internally according to polyarchy, and the levels as a whole are governed by hierarchy.

Given N, the total number of members of the organization, and k, the number of levels, we were able to define a quasi-lexicographic ordering of the resulting configurations, that is, the different distributions of members across the levels subject to some specified restriction. In this ordering the first configuration has a large base and a very slim top, while the last configuration is more evenly distributed and has a stocky appearance. With the assumption that the project under scrutiny is good, we prove that correctness increases moving towards the stocky configuration.

We define a measure that associates a value of loyalty to each configuration, based on the fact that each configuration implies a different career perspective as perceived by the individuals. The stronger is this perception, the higher is the loyalty. We show that loyalty decreases moving towards the stocky configuration.

To simplify, we assume that the payoff resulting from a correct decision is 0, while that for an incorrect decision is 1. We then define a cost relative to the time required to take the decision. The sum of these two costs, in expected terms, measures efficiency. More flexibility is obtained by introducing a parameter which weighs the influence of loyalty. As a result, we studied and compared the efficiency of the configurations as a function of this parameter.

We can sum up the main results as follows. The stocky configuration is the most efficient when this parameter is 0. As this parameter increases, there is no configuration uniformly superior to the others (with respect to the individual probability p), but the dominant configurations are to be found among those of the stocky type. Further increases of the parameter cause a progressive shift of dominance towards the slim configurations. For sufficiently large values of the parameter, the first configuration (the slimmest one) appears to be the most efficient for almost all p values, except for values very close to 0.

The figure of the leader plays an important role in our analysis. Since the leader possesses a greater probability of choosing correctly (due to his past experience) he has the power to convince the other members of the organization to adhere to his choice. In general, the stronger is the leadership, the more rapid is the choice made by the organization, and viceversa. Thus, the leader may contribute to the reduction of time required to reach a decision. The presence of the leader allows a distinction - following Mènard (1994) - between authority and hierarchy contingent on command. The leader possesses authority, since he is able to convince the other members of the decision structure, but convinces others by means of his own reputation (based on his skills), and not necessarily through the hierarchical role within the organization. Within a hierarchy, on the other hand, each hierarch chooses through the right of command attributed to him. A hierarch is not necessarily a leader. The role and the consequences of the presence of a leader within a hierarchical decision structure represent ample material for further research.

Within pyramid and hierarchical decision structures, the top hierarch has the right and the duty to assess and to choose (in the sense of approving or not) the alternatives already approved by all the precedent decision levels. In our analysis we have considered simple pyramid decision structures, whereby the hierarch is the top manager of a unique decision structure made up of a number of decision levels. Actually, the top hierarch may be the arrival point of a decision made by different hierarchical decision structures working in parallel. Within each level of the different hierarchical decision structures, the choices can be reached through different decision rules (each decision level can choose, for example, according to polyarchy, with different majority rules). Apart from the decisions made by all the precedent levels, the top hierarch has the final word over the alternatives presented to him. In such an environment, at least two problems arise which are worth mentioning: the cost of communication of the information to the top hierarch, and the possibility of a clog in the communication stream to the top hierarch, which entails a delay in the decision and may have negative consequences on that decision. So the problem is to build a model for a hierarchical organization which is capable of minimizing both the cost of information processing, and the time necessary for the top manager to assess the received information.

REFERENCES

Akerlof G.A., 1983, Loyalty filters, *American Economic Review*, Vol. 73.

Alchian A. and H. Demsetz, 1972, Production, information costs and economic organization, *American Economic Review*, Vol. 62.

Alchian A. and S. Woodward, 1988, The firm is dead. Long live the firm, *Journal of Economic Literature*, Vol. 26.

Andreoni J., 1991, Reasonable Doubt and Optimal Magnitude of Fines: Should the Penalty Fit the Crime?, *Rand Journal of Economics*, Vol. 22.

Arrow K.J., 1985, The economics of agency, in: John W. Pratt and Richard J. Zeckhauser, eds., *Principals and agents: the structure of business*, Harvard Business School Press, Boston.

Bendor J., 1985, *Parallel systems: redundancy in government*, University of California Press, Berkeley and Los Angeles.

Berg S., 1993a, Condorcet's Jury Theorem, Dependency among Jurors, *Social Choice and Welfare*, Vol. 10.

Berg S., 1993b, Condorcet's Jury Theorem Revisited, *European Journal of Political Economy*, Vol. 9.

Berg S., 1994, Evaluation of some weighted majority decision rules under dependent voting, *Mathematical Social Sciences*, Vol. 28.

Boland P.J., 1989, Majority systems and the Condorcet jury theorem, *The statisticien*, Vol. 38.

Boland P.J., Proschan F. and Y.L. Tong, 1989, Modelling dependence in simple and indirect majority systems, *Journal of Applied Probability*, Vol. 26.

Bowles S., 1985, The production process in a competitive economy: walrasian, neo-Hobbesian and marxian models, *American Economic Review*, Vol. 75.

Bull C. and J.A. Ordover, 1987, Market structure and optimal management organizations, *Rand Journal of Economics*, Vol. 18.

Calvo, G.A., 1985, The inefficiency of unemployment: the supervision perspective, *Quarterly Journal of Economics*, Vol.

100.

Catalani M.S., 1993, Transition Times in a First Order Homogeneous Markov Chain with Denumerable States: Some Matrix Form Algorithms, in *Some Results in Matrix Theory, with Applications to Selected Problems of Econometrics, Mimeo*, Dipartimento di Economia, Torino.

Catalani M.S. and Clerico G.F., 1993, Team cooperation or independent assessment?, *Riv. Inter. di Scienze Economiche e Commerciali*, Vol. 40.

Catalani M.S. and Clerico G.F., 1993, Pyramid structures in the decision process: a preliminary note, *Riv. Inter. di Scienze Economiche e Commerciali*, Vol. 40.

Catalani, Mario S. e Giuseppe F. Clerico, 1994, Processo decisionale e burocrazia: una rassegna sui problemi della fallibilita' delle decisioni delle istituzioni (Decision process and bureaucracy: a survey on the problems of the fallibility of the decisions of the institutions), in: Giuseppe Sobbrio, ed., *Modelli organizzativi e intervento pubblico*, Giuffre', Milano.

Catalani M.S. and Clerico G.F., 1995, How and When Unanimity is a Superior Decision Rule, *Riv. Inter. di Scienze Economiche e Commerciali*, Vol. 42.

Coase R., 1937, The nature of the firm, *Economica*, Vol. 2.

Cox D.R. and D.V. Hinkley, 1994, *Theoretical Statistics*, Chapman and Hall, London.

Fama E. and M.C. Jensen, 1983, Separation of ownership and control, *Journal of Law and Economics*, Vol. 26.

Feller W., 1968, *An Introduction to Probability Theory and Its Applications, Vol. I*, 3rd Edition, Wiley and Sons, New York, N.Y.

Gantmacher F.R., 1974, *The Theory of Matrices, Vol. I and II*, Chelsea Publishing Company, New York, N.Y.

Groot M.H., 1970, *Optimal Statistical Decisions*, McGraw-Hill, New York, N.Y.

Hayek F. von, 1945, The use of knowledge in society, *American Economic Review*, Vol. 35.

Hirschman A.O., 1970, *Exit, voice, and loyalty*, Harvard University Press, Cambridge, Ma.

Holmstrom B., 1979, Moral hazard and observability, *Bell Journal of Economics*, Vol. 10.

Holmstrom B., 1982, Moral hazard in teams, *Bell Journal of Economics*, Vol. 13.

Karotkin D., 1993, Inferiority of restricted majority decision rules, *Public Choice*, Vol. 77.

Koh Winston T.H., 1992, Human Fallibility and Sequential Decision Making: Hierarchy versus Polyarchy, *Journal of Economic Behaviour and Organization*, Vol. 18.

Klevorick A.K. and M. Rothschild, 1979, A Model of the Jury Decision Process, *Journal of Legal Studies*, Vol. 8.

Klevorick A.K., Rothschild M. and C. Winship, 1984, Information Processing and Jury Decisionmaking, *Journal of Public Economics*, Vol. 23.

Levinthal D., 1988, A survey of agency models of organizations, *Journal of Economic Behavior and Organization*, Vol. 9.

Loève M., 1978, *Probability Theory II*, 4th Ed., Springer-Verlag, New York, N.Y.

March J.G. and H.A. Simon, 1993, *Organizations*, 2nd Ed., Blackwell Publishers, Oxford.

Ménard C., 1994, Organizations as coordinating devices, *Metroeconomica*, Vol. 45.

Miller G.J., 1992, *Managerial dilemmas, the political economy of hierarchy*, Cambridge University Press, Cambridge, Ma.

Nitzan S. and J. Paroush, 1982, Optimal decision rules in uncertain dichotomous choice situations, *International Economic Review*, Vol. 23.

Nitzan S. and J. Paroush, 1984, Are qualified majority rules special?, *Public Choice*, Vol. 42.

Nitzan S. and U. Procaccia, 1986, Optimal Voting Procedures for Profit Maximizing Firms, *Public Choice*, Vol. 51.

Pauly M.V., 1968, The economics of moral hazard: comment, *American Economic Review*, Vol. 58.

Radner R., 1992, Hierarchy: the economics of managing, *Journal of Economic Literature*, Vol. 30.

Rees, Ray, 1985a, The theory of principal and agent, Part I, *Bulletin of Economic Research*, Vol. 37.

Rees, Ray, 1985b, The theory of principal and agent, Part II, *Bulletin of Economic Research*, Vol. 37.

Rényi A., 1970, *Foundations of Probability*, Holden Day, San Francisco, Ca.

Ross S., 1973, The economic theory of agency: the principal's problem, *American Economic Review*, Vol. 63.

Sah R.K., 1991, Fallibility in human organizations and political systems, *Journal of Economic Perspectives*, Vol. 5.

Sah R.K. and J.E. Stiglitz, 1985, Human Fallibility and Economic Organization, *American Economic Review, Papers and Proceedings*, Vol. 75.

Sah R.K. and J.E. Stiglitz, 1986, The Architecture of Economic Systems: Hierarchies and Poliarchies, *American Economic Review*, Vol. 76.

Sah R.K. and J.E. Stiglitz, 1988a, *Human Fallibility and Economic Organizations*, MIT Press, Cambridge, Ma.

Sah R.K. and J.E. Stiglitz, 1988b, Committees, Hierarchies and Poliarchies, *Economic Journal*, Vol. 98.

Sah R.K. and J.E. Stiglitz, 1991, The Quality of Managers in Centralized versus Decentralized Organizations, *Quarterly Journal of Economics*, Vol. VI, 1991.

Shapiro C. and J.E. Stiglitz, 1984, Equilibrium unemployment as a worker incentive device, *American Economic Review*, Vol. 74.

Shapley L. and B. Grofman, Optimizing group judgemental accuracy in the presence of interdependencies, *Public Choice*, Vol. 43.

Shavell S., 1979, Risk sharing and incentives in the principal and agent relationship, *Bell Journal of Economics*, Vol. 10.

Simon H.A., 1991, Organizations and markets, *Journal of Economic Perspectives*, Vol. 5.

Stiglitz J.E., 1974, Incentives and risk sharing in sharecropping, *Review of Economic Studies*, Vol. 41.

Weitzman M.L., 1984, *The share economy. Conquering stagflation*, Harvard University Press, Cambridge, Ma.

Williamson O.E., 1975, *Markets and hierarchies*, Free Press, New York.